GUIDED ASTROLOGY WORKBOOK

GUIDED ASTROLOGY WORKBOOK

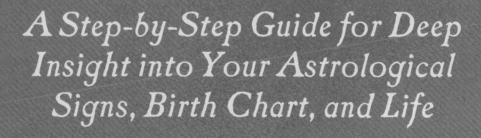

A Step-by-Step Guide for Deep Insight into Your Astrological Signs, Birth Chart, and Life

....

STEFANIE CAPONI

ILLUSTRATED BY Coni Curi

Zeitgeist • New York

For everyone who has lovingly put up with my incessant astrology chatter over the years, especially my wonderful husband, Kevin

. . . .

Published in the United States by Zeitgeist, an imprint of Zeitgeist™, a division of Penguin Random House LLC, New York.
zeitgeistpublishing.com

Zeitgeist™ is a trademark of Penguin Random House LLC
ISBN: 9780593690543

Illustrations by Coni Curi
Earth image on page 14 © by Very_Very/Shutterstock;
asteroid symbols on page 154 © by 3xy/Shutterstock
Book design by Emma Hall
Illustrator photo © 2020 by Ignacio Sanchez
Edited by Meg Ilasco and Sarah Curley

Printed in China
2nd Printing

Contents

INTRODUCTION

In my teens and twenties, glossy magazines reigned supreme. Just like everyone I knew, I subscribed to multiple fashion and beauty monthlies and eagerly awaited their arrival in my mailbox. My favorite part? Reading the horoscopes. I read at least six different columns to see what advice the stars held for me each month. Sometimes they resonated, but other times I felt a disconnect. As a Leo Sun sign, these articles often painted me as an endlessly sparkly, outgoing, and theatrical person. I sparkled sometimes, but not every single day.

Then in my midthirties, every part of my life fell apart at the same time. My marriage ended without explanation. I quit my job and gave away everything I owned to drive across the country with a couple of suitcases and zero plans. It was then that I turned to the stars for support and received my first professional astrology reading, hoping it would provide me with much-needed guidance. It did not disappoint.

The astrologer I hired sent me a detailed audio file along with my natal chart. (A natal chart is basically a snapshot of the stars based on the exact day, time, and place you were born. "Natal" means "related to the time or place of birth," which is why these charts are sometimes called "birth charts.") I must have listened to that recording more than a hundred times, soaking up all the insights it revealed. The first big aha moment came when I learned that I was so much more than my Leo Sun sign; the disconnect I'd felt from those monthly magazine horoscopes finally made sense. There was far more going on in my chart than just big, bold Leo energy—and each time I listened to the audio, I became more convinced that I needed to understand the subtleties of the cryptic chart that came with it.

I tried reading a handful of astrology books, but I found astrology blogs and YouTube videos far more helpful. I focused on learning about the planets and houses first before moving on to more complex stuff like aspects and asteroids. With patience and practice, I was able to connect the dots and read my birth chart with ease. By diving even deeper into the details, I discovered that my passions could become more than just hobbies if I chose to turn them into a new career. I also learned what I truly needed from my partnerships: romantic, platonic, and in business. The most healing part of this exploratory process was gaining insight into and understanding around my childhood experiences. This unexpected tool for personal growth allowed me to make peace with my upbringing and release resentments I had held tightly for too long.

Learning to read my birth chart wasn't as hard as I thought it would be, which is one reason I'm excited to show you how to do it yourself. Since your birth chart represents the positions of stars and planets at the exact moment of your birth, it looks like a pie chart that's divided into 12 pieces. Those are called "houses," with one for each topic or area of life. (More on this soon. Promise.) Your Sun sign, Moon sign, Ascendant sign, and eight planets are sprinkled throughout the houses in your chart. Each planet and house has a general meaning that will become specific to you based on how it is positioned in your chart, like a map of your personality, ambitions, hidden desires, and fundamental needs.

Knowing how to read your birth chart is the gift that keeps on giving. When you become familiar with it, you'll quickly see that astrology can help guide you toward self-understanding, personal growth, and spiritual development. It can even help answer questions like *What am I good at? What do I really want to do with my life?* and *What was the purpose of my most painful moments, and what were they leading me toward?* Astrology allows us to understand ourselves on a cosmic level, but it can also help with more earthly matters like navigating the layers and nuances of interpersonal relationships. The secrets to unlocking your inner world and discovering your greatest potential are in these pages, and I can't wait for you to dive in.

A BRIEF HISTORY OF ASTROLOGY

Most of us know that astrology has to do with stars and planets and things that were happening in outer space the moment each of us was born, but how do we actually define it? What *is* astrology?

Astrology is the 2,000-year-old study of the movement of celestial objects and how those movements influence our bodies, lives, and the natural world. It's commonly used to forecast future events as well as find resonance in events from the past, within our personal lives, our families, and world events throughout history.

Now considered a pseudoscience and categorized as a form of divination, astrology was once held in high regard alongside astronomy, alchemy, meteorology, and medicine. Historically famous astronomers like Galileo and Kepler served at court, advising royalty on how the stars might impact their reigns. Astrology was used by many cultures around the world—including those of the Mayans, Indians, Chinese, Egyptians, Greeks, and Romans—to predict seasonal shifts and foretell divine prophecies. Tracking lunar cycles and the times of year when constellations could be seen also influenced how each culture built their calendar system.

Astrology as we know it today is a hybrid of several much older practices. It began to take shape during the Hellenistic period in Greece in the fourth century BCE, blend-ing elements of Babylonian astrology and Egyptian decanic astrology. (Decans were 36 individual stars or small constellations that rose and set at different times of the year. The Egyptians used these to understand their world and make predictions.) Western astrology—based mainly on the famous Greek astrologer Ptolemy's second-century CE work, *Tetrabiblos*, a text on the philosophy and practice of astrology that evolved from Hellenistic astrology—is widely practiced in the English-speaking countries of the world, and it's the style that you will use in this book.

GETTING YOUR BIRTH CHART

Before you dive any deeper into this book, you will need a copy of your birth chart. My favorite charts to work with come from astro.com, which has been around for many years. An internet search for "free natal chart calculation" should lead you to any number of other tools if astro.com doesn't work for you.

Most free websites default to the time-based Placidus system, devised during the Renaissance, to calculate the houses. I suggest using the Placidus system as you begin your astrological journey and study other methods once you are familiar with reading your chart. To find your birth chart on Astro.com, follow the steps below. (These instructions were accurate at time of writing, but you may need to make minor adjustments if the site has gotten a face-lift.)

- Visit Astro.com and select "Horoscopes" from the task bar.
- Under the dropdown heading "Drawings, Calculations, Data," select "Chart Drawing, Ascendant" (or "Extended Chart Selection" to add additional asteroids).
- Follow the prompts to populate each field with your birth data. Ideally, you should include your birth time (down to the minute) and birthplace.
- Voilà, you now have your birth chart! You can print it out to follow alongside this workbook or save the image to preserve it in digital form.

WHAT AM I LOOKING AT?

To orient yourself with your chart, first look for a box that lists all of your natal placements. It may look like gibberish now—with notations like *Sun 27 Cap 30'35"* and *Neptune 15 Sag 11'45"*—but see what you can glean. You can probably tell that "Cap" means Capricorn and "Sag" means Sagittarius. This box tells you the placements of your Sun, Moon, Mercury, Venus, Mars, Jupiter, Saturn, Uranus, Neptune, Pluto, North Node (sometimes referred to as "True Node," depending on the astrology website consulted), Chiron, Ascendant (AC), and Midheaven (MC) signs within the 12 houses. These are all of the stars, planets, and celestial bodies that we use to understand our charts. The numbers next to each sign are the degrees of each placement, and we'll learn about that later.

You should also see a box with a list of planets (it may look like a table of hieroglyphics) and some intersecting lines on your birth chart. These aspect lines and symbols represent the many ways the planets in your unique chart are talking to one another. In astrology, the relationship between two or more planets in your birth chart are represented by the lines that make zigzag patterns. Each of these lines represents the three basic types of aspects: harmonious, challenging, and conjunctions. (More on these in the chapters to come.)

WHAT IF I DON'T KNOW MY BIRTH TIME?

I promise you can still benefit from working with your birth chart! If you select "unknown" when entering your birth time information, you'll get a chart without any lines because time is needed to make the mathematical calculations that reveal your Ascendant sign and the houses where each planet falls. But here's the good news: all of your planets are still in their proper signs, so you can work with their energies and still learn plenty of valuable information about yourself.

LEARNING TO READ YOUR BIRTH CHART

Now the fun begins! This book will walk you through all the steps you must take to understand the many layers of information embedded in your unique birth chart.

Every aspect of astrology is connected, so it can be tricky to learn everything in a way that feels linear and logical . . . but here's how I've chosen to walk through it with you: we'll review the wheel and each house before moving one by one through each planetary placement. Then we'll take a look at some of the other aspects of your chart that will prompt you to dig even deeper into your understanding of not just astrology but yourself.

In each section, you'll learn new information that builds off the previous section, allowing you to integrate more and more of these elements into your understanding of astrology. You will find exercises and reflections to aid in the integration process as you dive deeper into connecting to your birth chart and discovering more about yourself in the process. There's also a blank birth chart on page 22 where you can view your wheel and fill in your details as you go for easy reference.

Let's begin!

ONE

Understanding the Zodiac Wheel

· ·

THE ONLY WAY to understand *your* birth chart is to understand how *all* birth charts are calculated—and to make that possible, the first concept you'll need to master is the zodiac.

The zodiac is a mythical band in the sky that roughly follows the ecliptic: the path the Sun takes across the sky over the course of a calendar year. Imagine a giant belt out in space that's covered in stars and planets. It's got the Sun and Moon on it, every planet in our solar system, and the 12 constellations of stars that make up the astrological signs. Since the ecliptic is a big, unbroken belt, the Sun travels along it in a never-ending cycle that repeats every 12 months. (It's really the Earth that's orbiting the Sun, of course, but the entire system of astrology was created from an Earthbound perspective. And down here, what we see is the Sun moving around that big imaginary belt in the sky.) These 12 signs—Aries, Taurus, Gemini, Cancer, Leo, Virgo, Libra, Scorpio, Sagittarius, Capricorn, Aquarius, and Pisces—are spaced equally along the surface of the belt 30 degrees apart from each other.

Wherever the Sun happened to be sitting on that belt in the moment of your birth defines your Sun sign, which is the tiny sliver of astrology covered in most horoscopes. It's important, but it's only one aspect of your chart.

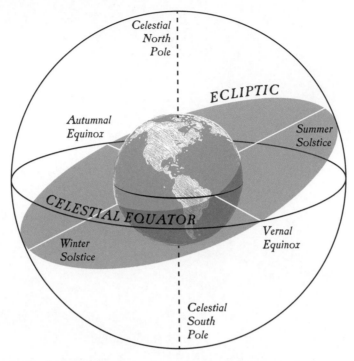

A CYCLICAL PATTERN

The zodiac and constellations interact with each other in cycles. Their movement is visibly tied to the ecliptic of the Sun across the sky during the year. And since the belt of the zodiac and the pie pieces of the houses look like an old-fashioned wagon wheel, we often refer to this cyclical system as the "zodiac wheel."

Each of the 12 astrological signs gets to rule one of the 12 houses, based on the time of year each constellation is visible in the sky. Houses are the pie pieces you see on your chart, and their names are their numbers. The First House is ruled by Aries; the Second House is ruled by Taurus; and so on around the cycle of astrological signs until we get to the Twelfth House, which is ruled by Pisces. Each house represents a key aspect of life, from health and money to relationships and communication. You can think of the houses like a map of the big circle of sky that sits in the middle of the zodiac belt, with the planets constantly moving from house to house. When you were born, each planet was hanging out in a particular house, and you can see which one by looking at your birth chart. Each planet's position in a specific house will impact your life and personality!

If you place your birth chart next to the natural zodiac wheel below, you will notice that the natural wheel differs from your personal chart based on your individual Ascendant sign. Aries rules the First House, but if you're an Aquarius rising, Aquarius will be your Ascendant sign *and* ruler of your First House. But regardless of your personal house rulers, each house has the energy of its natural ruler. To keep things simple here, let's take a look at the zodiac wheel with each house's natural ruler. Doing this will help you understand the energy and meaning of each house and its ruling sign when you begin to analyze your birth chart.

As we develop and mature, we will experience different aspects of each house. When we're in our twenties and lots of cosmic action hits the Fifth House, we may feel exhilarated. When those same celestial bodies align in the Fifth House and we're in our fifties, we may interpret those energies in profound new ways. The zodiac wheel serves as a cyclical roadmap of our lives, with each house offering us insight into how we may feel or act at different stages and ages.

ZODIAC SIGN CHARACTERISTICS

Just like real people, the zodiac signs are complex. They've got personalities and opinions and unique ways of behaving, all of which help make them robust and nuanced characters. Much of that nuance comes from the layers of symbology and association that each sign contains. So, let's excavate some layers, shall we?

Each of the zodiac signs is represented by a mythological character or archetype. These are the symbols you likely know already: the crab for Cancer, the twins for Gemini, the scorpion for Scorpio, etc.

You can think of the archetype as the simplest way of understanding a sign. The archetypical symbols give some general clues to how each sign will behave. Leo's archetype is the lion, which means Leos are known for their leadership skills and bravery, while Libra's archetype is the scales of justice, which means Libras tend to be fair-minded and value balance. These archetypes are just the broad strokes you might find in a horoscope column, but they're important concepts to understand. Along with these easily recognizable symbols, each sign is also associated with some important groups of characteristics:

Dualities: Astrological duality has to do with how much masculine and feminine energy each sign expresses. This is not related to the concepts of gender that exist today; it's simply used to describe how each sign expresses their energy. In the context of astrology, masculine energy, or yang, is assertive, structured, and action-oriented, while the feminine, or yin, is intuitive, receptive, and flowing.

Elements: Each sign is associated with one of the four main elements: Earth, air, fire, or water. This elemental association influences how the sign behaves. You may have heard someone say that they're a "water sign." They're referring to the element that's paired with their Sun sign.

Modalities: These are also called the three qualities: cardinal, fixed, and mutable. Cardinal signs are associated with initiation and creativity; fixed signs are associated with determination and individuality; mutable signs are associated with adaptability and resourcefulness.

SIGN	HOUSE NUMBER	SYMBOL/ GLYPH	ARCHETYPE
ARIES	1st House	♈	The Ram
TAURUS	2nd House	♉	The Bull
GEMINI	3rd House	♊	The Twins
CANCER	4th House	♋	The Crab
LEO	5th House	♌	The Lion
VIRGO	6th House	♍	The Virgin
LIBRA	7th House	♎	The Scales of Justice
SCORPIO	8th House	♏	The Scorpion
SAGITTARIUS	9th House	♐	The Archer
CAPRICORN	10th House	♑	The Sea Goat
AQUARIUS	11th House	♒	The Water Bearer
PISCES	12th House	♓	The Fish

Taking your knowledge a step further to puzzle out dualities, elements, and modalities will deepen the flavor of each sign, giving it more range and texture. Just like us, these signs are all multidimensional beings and cannot be distilled down to a few key words and simple symbols.

DUALITIES

As humans, we love to oversimplify complex feelings and ideas into simple binaries. Our brains are hardwired to categorize things as "right" or "wrong" for ease rather than acknowledging the gray areas that often make up our reality. But the truth is that many choices we make have a little bit of right and a little bit of wrong in them. Every person has some light and some dark—or some yin and some yang—in them. Duality is a fundamental part of life. It's also part of nature, and it helps our world stay balanced.

SIGN	DUALITY
ARIES	Masculine
TAURUS	Feminine
GEMINI	Masculine
CANCER	Feminine
LEO	Masculine
VIRGO	Feminine
LIBRA	Masculine
SCORPIO	Feminine
SAGITTARIUS	Masculine
CAPRICORN	Feminine
AQUARIUS	Masculine
PISCES	Feminine

Now, think of astrology as a world that's populated by the astrological signs. The polar dualities in astrology give each sign the title of masculine or feminine to maintain balance in that world. This does not assign gender to any sign. When we refer to a sign's dualities as masculine or feminine, we are using those terms to describe the energy of a person with that sign and how that person might interact with other people and in their environments. Masculine energy encompasses traits typically associated with yang: assertive, structured, and action-oriented, while the feminine yin is intuitive, receptive, and flowing. One is neither better nor worse than the other, and each sign craves balance and duality, just as we all do, using both energies within us to embody our richest, most wholesome lives.

The signs in the table are listed in the order in which they arise throughout the calendar year. Notice how they alternate, beginning with Aries/masculine. This should help you remember that dualities are alternating in order to maintain balance.

 ## GENDERED LANGUAGE IN ASTROLOGY

Astrology is an ancient practice that continues to use the terms "masculine" and "feminine" to describe the duality and polarity of the signs and planets. While these terms are often associated with particular genders today, they are not associated with gender in astrology. "Feminine" and "masculine" have been used throughout time by various cultures to describe dual energies. This was popularized in the West by psychologist Carl Jung. The signs have not been assigned a gender; rather, when you read about Venus being feminine and Mars being masculine, it means the energy of these planets is being expressed in a way traditionally associated with the energies of the "feminine" and "masculine." These terms could also be replaced with "yin" and "yang."

ELEMENTS

The four elements play roles in the belief systems of countless cultures across time and space. Like the dualities, the elements (earth, air, fire, and water) help create harmony and balance in our world. Some conceptualize them as the foundations of life as we know it: to survive, we need the soil beneath our feet, the water we drink, the air we breathe, and the power that fire lends us. Learning the elemental associations of each zodiac sign will help you connect with their core essence.

Fire signs (Aries, Leo, Sagittarius) are known to be passionate, creative, assertive, and reactionary. They're the quickest sign to jump into action mode, sometimes before thinking things through.

Earth signs (Taurus, Virgo, Capricorn) move slowly and deliberately, weighing all options before taking action. They're known to be steady, grounded, sensual, and in tune with their bodies.

Air signs (Gemini, Libra, Aquarius) are quick-witted, both flighty and deep thinkers. They're excellent communicators but tend to overthink or intellectualize before taking action.

Water signs (Cancer, Scorpio, Pisces) are intuitive, known for their depth of emotions. They tend to experience the world through their complex feelings, looking for safety before taking action.

MODALITIES

Not all fire signs are created equal. That goes for earth, air, and water signs, too! This is where modalities swoop in to add depth to each sign. Think of it this way: the element lays the groundwork for a sign and the modality builds on it, giving it even more character and purpose. For example, there are three fire signs: Aries, Leo, and Sagittarius. Aries is a cardinal fire sign, Leo is a fixed fire sign, and Sagittarius is a mutable fire sign.

Every element is represented in each modality, creating quadruplicities (or a set of four signs).

Cardinal signs (Aries, Cancer, Libra, Capricorn) are initiators. They're the ones most likely to get the party started. These signs are here to be leaders and forge new paths.

Fixed signs (Taurus, Leo, Scorpio, Aquarius) are immovable when they have made their minds up. Change may be challenging for these signs, but finishing what they've started is their specialty. They are here to model fortitude and longevity.

Mutable signs (Gemini, Virgo, Sagittarius, Pisces) are all about evolution. They are the most flexible group of signs and offer us shining examples of growth when they are given the leeway to change and adapt.

SIGN	ELEMENT	MODALITY
ARIES	Fire	Cardinal
TAURUS	Earth	Fixed
GEMINI	Air	Mutable
CANCER	Water	Cardinal
LEO	Fire	Fixed
VIRGO	Earth	Mutable
LIBRA	Air	Cardinal
SCORPIO	Water	Fixed
SAGITTARIUS	Fire	Mutable
CAPRICORN	Earth	Cardinal
AQUARIUS	Air	Fixed
PISCES	Water	Mutable

Complete the Zodiac Wheel

1. Within the inner wheel, number the houses 1–12, moving counterclockwise from the left horizon line marked "AC" for Ascendant.

2. Along the outermost wheel, fill in the naturally ruling zodiac sign for each house (see page 15), beginning with Aries.

3. In the largest section of the wheel, draw the glyph (see page 17) that is associated with each sign.

AC

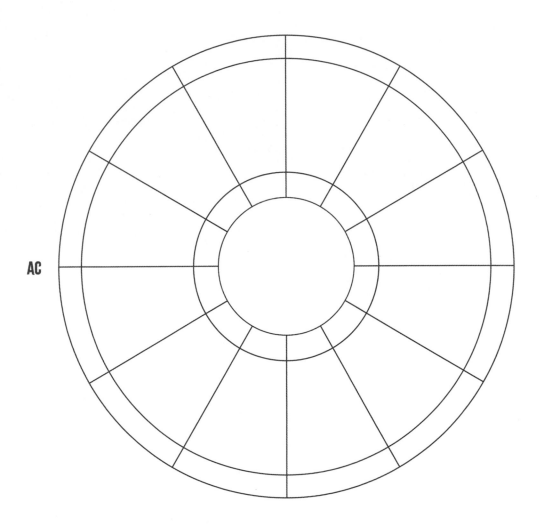

Working with My Birth Chart: The Big Three

1. Fill in your Big Three below. Next to each sign, write down the element, modality, and duality of each sign.

    Sun in ....Element........................Modality ....Duality ....

    Moon in ....Element........................Modality ....Duality ....

    Ascendant in ....Element........................Modality ....Duality ....

2. How similar or different do these qualities seem?

    ....

    ....

    ....

REFLECTION

What insights arise as you study the contrast of each sign's varying characteristics? Look at where each of these are located on your birth chart. Are they close to one another? Far apart? Near the top of your chart or the bottom? Are you beginning to see how these components are vital to understanding the wonderful complexities that comprise you?

....

....

....

TWO

Exploring the 12 Houses

· · · · · · · · · · · · · · · · · · · ·

YOU CAN TELL a lot about a person by looking at their house. One person's home might be overflowing with plants, books, and knickknacks, while another's might be stark and bare. Some people constantly change the decor or repaint the walls of their home, while others leave everything the same for decades. Objects, colors, layout, scents, shapes, and amount of clutter all hint at the inhabitant's habits and traits. Even doing nothing is a choice that's reflected in their living space.

The same goes for the houses in the zodiac! These segments of the wheel are a critically important part of your birth chart, and when you start studying which planets land in which houses, you'll get a whole new perspective on your identity. Some of your personal planetary placements may fall in several houses, or predominantly in one or two, leaving some houses empty. This doesn't mean those empty houses aren't very important in your chart; rather, this means that the houses that contain your planets are going to see more action over the course of a lifetime, whereas the other houses will have important significance from time to time through planetary transits. For the purpose of becoming proficient at analyzing your birth chart, we are not focusing on transits in this book.

The houses of the zodiac reflect 12 areas of life that we cycle through again and again as we grow and mature over the course of our lifetimes. As you get older, your life naturally evolves in the areas of knowledge, family, love, relationships, finance, and your contribution to the planet. Your natal planets will fall in certain houses, sprinkling the flavor of the house into the essence of the planet in any given sign. Knowing and understanding the similarities and differences of the natural rulers and your own rulers for each of the 12 houses will help you gain a deeper understanding of your own personality, patterns, and life experiences.

Before we explore the planets specific to your birth chart, we need to become familiar with each of the 12 houses and their general meanings. This will ensure that when you look at any birth chart—not just your own—you'll understand what the wheel is all about.

THE FIRST HOUSE

NATURAL RULER: Aries

KEY WORDS: appearance; first impressions

AFFIRMATION: I am a multifaceted individual, here to make my mark on the world.

The First House is naturally ruled by Aries. This is the house of You™; the version of yourself that the world sees. It is your outward physical appearance, the first impressions you make, and how people perceive you. The First House is also known as the mask you wear to move stealthily through the world to achieve the mission of your Sun sign. In some ways it reflects your approach to life more than your essential core identity.

Soon we'll talk about planetary associations for each zodiac sign, since each sign is linked to a planet in our solar system. But for now, a quick preview: the planet that rules the zodiac sign on the cusp of your first house is also known as your chart ruler (see page 33 for more on cusps). The special title of "chart ruler" is assigned to the planetary ruler of your First House and plays a special role in your role in life, working in tandem with your Sun sign to assist you in unfolding your birth chart's gifts and shaping how the world sees you.

THE SECOND HOUSE

NATURAL RULER: Taurus

KEY WORDS: possessions; values; self-esteem

AFFIRMATION: I value myself; I am worthy of all of the good that life has to offer.

The Second House is the house of your values, self-worth, and possessions and is naturally ruled by Taurus. The sign on the cusp of your Second House can indicate your sense of worthiness and self-esteem, as well as your attitude about money, how possessive you are about things and people in your life, and what you value in the world. This house can give helpful clues about the best ways for you to earn money.

Is the Second House just reflecting your materialistic side? Not at all. What goes on in here is not limited to tangible things. After all, we own our feelings and emotions as well as our identities, abilities, needs, and wants. When we talk about "owning up" to something—like a secret desire or mistake we've made—it means we are claiming ownership of an element of our true selves. Neither ownership nor value can be boiled down to just money and things; think of the Second House as the place where what you appreciate and regard will reside.

THE THIRD HOUSE

NATURAL RULER: Gemini

KEY WORDS: communication; short trips; early learning

AFFIRMATION: When I open myself to multiple points of view, my wisdom constantly expands.

The Third House is the house of communication, mindset, the way you process information, your local community, short-distance travel, and your relationships with siblings and close relatives. Does that seem like a lot of things randomly packed together? That's because the Third House is naturally ruled by Gemini, and these all fall under Mercury's busy umbrella, since Mercury is the planet that rules Gemini.

The Third House also deals with early school years, and the sign on the cusp of this house in your birth chart gives valuable insight as to how you received information as a kid. Since family falls to this house as well, it may explain what your relationships with your siblings, cousins, aunts, and uncles were like. This is a foundational house of your mindset that describes how the ideas you internalized during your formative years have become your core beliefs—beliefs that will grow and evolve over the course of your lifetime.

THE FOURTH HOUSE

NATURAL RULER: Cancer

KEY WORDS: home; family; foundation of the chart

AFFIRMATION: No matter where I go, I am always at home within myself.

The Fourth House is a very important house since it forms the foundation of your psychological and emotional self. It's also known as the Imum Coeli (IC), meaning the nadir or bottom of your chart. Ruled by Cancer, the Fourth House is associated with parental care and the behaviors that were modeled to you in your formative years.

The sign connected to your Fourth House in your chart describes the type of childhood you had; how you thought and felt about your parents; the type of discipline and parental care you received; and anything that remains to be excavated in your subconscious. Learning about your Fourth House is the key to undertaking any inner-child healing work you might need, since this is a highly sensitive point in your chart.

THE FIFTH HOUSE

NATURAL RULER: Leo

KEY WORDS: pleasure; creativity; casual dating

AFFIRMATION: My sense of playfulness honors my individuality and creativity; I am here to shine.

The Fifth House is the house of playfulness, creativity, and pleasure. While the Fourth House teaches you about your family and how you grew up, the Fifth House focuses on your individuality, who you were as a child, and how your children (should you have them) will experience you as a parent. For many who become parents, children are a source of tremendous pleasure as well as a creative extension of themselves.

This house also reigns over casual dating and will give you clues about the type of people you find attractive. (Though not necessarily for the long term. You'll learn about that in the Seventh House!) Romance, romantic affairs, and emotional satisfaction all reside here. The Fifth House is naturally ruled by vivacious Leo, and this is the part of your chart where you shine, express yourself creatively, and are meant to stand out.

THE SIXTH HOUSE

NATURAL RULER: Virgo

KEY WORDS: daily routine; health; organization

AFFIRMATION: Prioritizing my well-being, developing healthy habits, and creating routines are all acts of self-care.

The Sixth House is the house of your physical health, daily routines, and your relationships with animals. Ruled by Virgo, this is the house where you balance your work responsibilities with how you structure your daily life; how you treat your body, organize your activities, and design your space. The mind-body connection is revealed through the way you balance these themes. The sign on the cusp of the Sixth House will give valuable clues about your work habits as well as how you take care of yourself physically.

Since health also encompasses resilience and our ability to deal with the unexpected, the Sixth House reflects these things. Crises, illness, and unfortunate surprises are all part of our lives. How will we confront these situations and deal with the lessons they want to teach us? Knowing this helps define the person we will become.

THE SEVENTH HOUSE

NATURAL RULER: Libra

KEY WORDS: balance; relationships; significant partnerships; marriage

AFFIRMATION: My relationships are mirrors, reflecting every part of my already whole and worthy self.

Ruled by Libra, the Seventh House is the house of significant partnerships and marriage (whatever that may mean to you). While the Fifth House describes casual dating experiences you might have, things get serious in the Seventh House. Partnerships can take many forms, as can marriages. (Some people say creative partners have a "marriage of minds"!) The essence of this house is about how you find people to complement you and how you choose to cooperate with them. Why do you seek the people you seek? How do you relate to them? Why are they the ones you want to love, work with, or collaborate with over the long term?

The Seventh House is also known as the "house of open enemies," which makes sense when we think about how painful and triggering some significant relationships can be. Ultimately, the sign on the cusp of the Seventh House will show you the qualities that you seek in a long-term partnership.

THE EIGHTH HOUSE

NATURAL RULER: Scorpio

KEY WORDS: sex; transformation; taboo subjects; hidden motivations

AFFIRMATION: I welcome transformation when I accept all hidden parts of myself without shame.

The Eighth House is where we merge with the "other," the partnerships that were forged in the Seventh House require vulnerability that include sexuality, combining finances, and revealing our secret selves. Ruled by Scorpio, the Eighth House is commonly known as the house of sex, death, and taxes.

Why death? The link between sex and death is often hearkened back to the French term for "orgasm," *le petit mort*, which means "little death." When we reach the apex of pleasure, we may sacrifice a little of ourselves or release it into the ether. Additionally, in many occult practices, there is a link between death and rebirth, growth, or new beginnings. The Eighth House wants us to know that sex, death, rebirth, and paying the price for what we desire are all equally important in life.

The sign connected to your Eighth House will reveal your sexual preferences, the type of marriage or long-term relationship you will have behind closed doors, your relationship to other people's money, any interest in occult studies, and all things considered taboo.

THE NINTH HOUSE

NATURAL RULER: Sagittarius

KEY WORDS: higher learning; long-distance travel; spirituality

AFFIRMATION: I expand my personal horizons when I open myself to new things. I will never stop growing as long as I am learning.

The Ninth House is the house of long-distance travel, higher education, and learning beyond what is taught in the classroom. This is the house of spiritual seekers, religious studies, and philosophy; anyone and everyone who quests for meaning in their lives. Ruled by Sagittarius, the Ninth House is where you go to broaden your horizons and explore new cultures.

This is also the house that rules publishing, teaching, and sharing your personal experiences the world has taught you. The sign connected to your Ninth House will offer clues about how you travel, experience new cultures, your religious or spiritual views, and possibly what you are here to share with the world.

THE TENTH HOUSE

NATURAL RULER: Capricorn

KEY WORDS: personal achievements; legacy; career apex

AFFIRMATION: My life's purpose is constantly unfolding. I delight in the journey rather than focusing on a destination.

The Tenth House is the house of meaningful work, your career, and the legacy you create in this lifetime. Ruled by Capricorn, the Tenth House is where you are highly motivated and focused to achieve your goals and leave your mark on the world. This is more than financial; it is what your soul longs to do to make the world a better place. It's also referred to as the "house of social status," since achievements, promotions, and fame always bring with them elevated social standing.

But generally, this is the house of work, vocation, and calling. What role do you want to carve out for yourself and how will you fill it? How much do you want to achieve now and in the future? Career, professional goals, ambition, and motivation all come into play here. The sign on the cusp of the Tenth House will help you understand your unique gifts that will help you make those dreams a reality.

THE ELEVENTH HOUSE

NATURAL RULER: Aquarius

KEY WORDS: friendships; group activities; hope for the future

AFFIRMATION: My role in society and my friendships are special. I'm confident sharing my unique perspective and ideas.

The Eleventh House is the house of social circles, friendships, groups you belong to, your hopes and dreams, and futuristic advancements for yourself and society. Ruled by Aquarius, the Eleventh House asks you to push yourself out of old comfort zones and look ahead to the future, to learn about and implement new technology, to come together with others in favor of the bigger picture, and to take your Tenth House achievements and share them with others.

The sign on the cusp of the Eleventh House will show you the type of friends you attract and how you show up in groups. It can also reveal how you will share your gifts and skills with the world.

THE TWELFTH HOUSE

NATURAL RULER: Pisces

KEY WORDS: dreams; self-undoing; escapism; universal oneness

AFFIRMATION: I realize my "unhealthy" habits are my strengths, and they are here to teach me how to help the collective.

The Twelfth House is a mysterious house that connects you to the collective unconscious. Ruled by Pisces, the Twelfth House is where your physical body meets your spiritual self and faces the struggle to be confined to a human body. Sometimes we feel bound and confined by our lives or stuck in a rut that we can't seem to break. This house is where we decide how we can move forward. Will we be honest and reveal hidden truths, or will we keep our secrets in the shadows?

The sign on the cusp of the Twelfth House will tell you how you self-sabotage by escaping reality. It can also show you the ways you experience suffering, isolation, imprisonment, and hidden enemies. (It's not as scary as it sounds.) This is where you can tap into the energy of the universe through dreams, meditation, music, art, and creativity. This house allows you to be a channel for higher forms of consciousness.

CUSPS

The house cusp is the line that marks the beginning of the house, like a door from the previous house to this house. From here on out, when we discuss the lines defining the end of one house and beginning of another house, we will refer to it as the cusp.

You may have also heard the term "cusp" referring to birthdays that fall close to the end of one sign and the beginning of another. For example, someone with a birthday on August 22 may consider themselves a Leo with "Virgo tendencies" because their birthday falls on the cusp of Virgo season. However, most astrologers do not recognize cusps in this manner due to the placement of other planets in one's natal chart. When we are talking about cusps in this workbook, we are strictly referring to the beginning of a particular house as it is used to determine house placement.

The 12 Houses

1. Write the zodiac sign that is the natural ruler of each of the 12 houses.

2. Label each house with key words to help you remember the important themes.

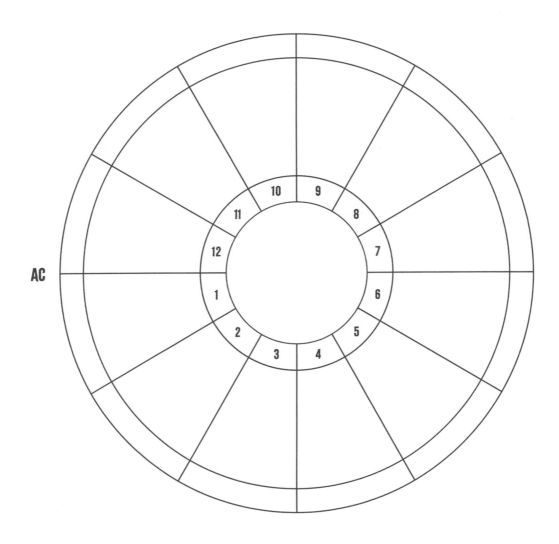

Working with My Birth Chart: House Rulers

1. Fill in the house rulers from your own birth chart and write the key words for each.

2. Think about the differences and similarities between the characteristics of the natural ruling signs versus the signs in your own chart.

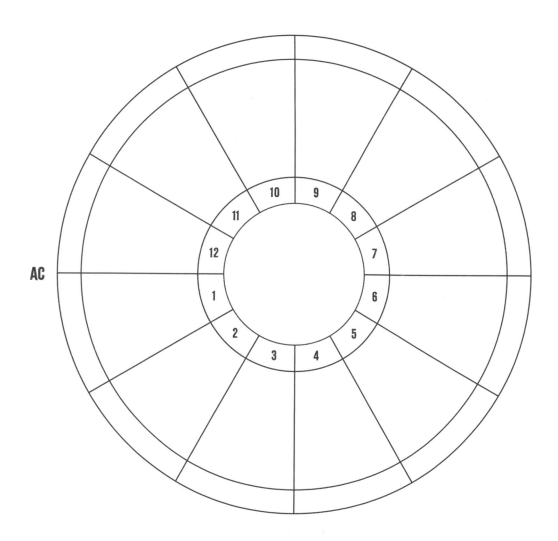

REFLECTION

First House: How do you think you are perceived as you move through the world?

....

....

....

Second House: What are some of the things you value most in life?

....

....

....

Third House: How did you experience school and learning when you were young?

....

....

....

Fourth House: What is something you appreciate about your childhood or family dynamic?

....

....

....

Fifth House: What is something you do to find joy or spark your creativity?

....

....

....

Sixth House: How do you approach your work environment and colleagues?

....

....

....

Seventh House: What are the qualities that draw you to a person?

....

....

....

Eighth House: How have you transformed throughout your life?

....

....

....

Ninth House: What is your dream trip or travel destination?

....

....

....

Tenth House: What are some ways you use or could use your natural gifts in your current career?

....

....

....

Eleventh House: Describe what happened the last time you stepped out of your comfort zone.

....

....

....

Twelfth House: What do you do to "escape" after a bad day?

....

....

....

THREE

Soaking Up the Sun Signs

· · · · · · · · · · · · · · · · · · · ·

THE SUN IS the brightest luminary in our solar system, the powerful star that makes our lives possible. Without its light and warmth, we would have no food, no environment, no way to thrive in this world. We may take it for granted, but the Sun helps us stay happy and healthy every single day of our lives.

Since the Sun is so important to life on Earth, it should be no surprise that it also plays an integral role in your birth chart! Your Sun sign is your primary zodiac sign because it represents your unique mission in this lifetime. It also encompasses your sense of self, romantic preferences, innate gifts, and the ways in which you move through the world. This is the reason so many horoscopes focus exclusively on Sun sign astrology: this sign defines your core personality and is paramount to understanding your identity. It may not be the only important aspect of your birth chart, but there's no doubt that it's a true pillar of your astrological self.

The sign and house in which your Sun resides in your birth chart will help you understand where you shine without effort. These placements will also help you embrace your most profound gifts and talents so you can share them with the world.

ARIES ♈

MARCH 21–APRIL 19

KEY WORDS

leader; initiator;
trailblazer

**ARIES
SEASON MANTRA**

Just do it.

Aries is the first sign of the zodiac and therefore the natural ruler of the First House. Aries is the cardinal fire sign ruled by Mars, the mythical god of war, symbolized by the ram and linked to the color red. These symbols are clues to the meaning and energy of Aries. Cardinal signs are associated with initiation; the element of fire and color red represent raw passion, and the first position indicates a specific kind of power. These are the hallmark traits of Aries.

Your Sun sign in Aries bestows you with immense drive and energy to initiate relationships, try new things, and forge new paths. You are here to lead others where no one has gone before. You might have a bit of a temper or be quick to argue. People may see you as a daredevil type or quick to jump into situations, but this is because they don't understand your innate instinct, knowing it's what you must do.

Ever notice how the world comes alive again in late March through early April? New classes begin at schools; the weather gets warmer; your energy miraculously returns as you get excited for spring. During the time of year when the Sun is transiting through Aries, the world and all of humanity receive a heavy dose of fiery Mars energy. This is when your Aries essence gets its yearly renewal, and you are tuned into the purest form of your personal power. It's the perfect time for initiating projects, taking action on ideas that have been in the planning stages, experimenting with new physical routines, dating new people, or joining new groups. The Aries season wants you to experience fresh starts that will get you excited for your life in new ways.

All about Aries

Using the information you've learned about Aries, fill in the table below. Creating a table of information for yourself will help you connect to the essence of Aries and understand its significant correlation with the First House.

HOUSE NUMBER IN THE ZODIAC	SYMBOL	DATES	
		RULING PLANET	
STRENGTHS		WEAKNESSES	
DUALITY		ELEMENT	COLOR
MODALITY			

TAURUS ♉

KEY WORDS
possessive;
traditional; sensual

**TAURUS
SEASON MANTRA**
Go toward what
feels good.

Taurus is the second sign of the zodiac and therefore the natural ruler of the Second House. Taurus is the fixed earth sign ruled by Venus, mythical goddess of love and beauty, symbolized by the bull and associated with the color green. These symbols will help give you clues to the obstinate yet sensual nature of Taurus. Since fixed signs are known for being stubborn, a bull can get angry when pushed toward uninvited change. However, beautiful Venus ensures the Taurus Sun's refinement, making them ultimate seekers of beauty and pleasure with no ill will or ulterior motives.

Your Sun in Taurus asks you to uphold your strong ideals and revel in your sense of beauty. These traits reveal themselves in an elevated taste for food and drink, fine furnishings, and creating a sense of comfort so you can escape from what is out of your control. Others may find you romantically alluring, yet you yourself find it difficult to commit. This isn't because you are afraid of commitment, but rather that you're not in a rush. You have patience for the process and don't make hasty decisions.

The Sun's yearly transit through Taurus is during the height of spring, when flowers are blooming, romance is in the air, and everyone is feeling generally indulgent. This is when schoolchildren get spring break, no one wants to work, and it's time for vacation and rest. The collective is experiencing a dose of decadent Venus energy, and your Taurus Sun is getting its yearly reset. This is the perfect time of year to take a break from the frenetic pace of Aries season and stop to smell the roses. Focus on your body, feeding yourself nourishing foods, prioritizing pleasure as self-care, and enjoying nature.

All about Taurus

Using the information you've learned about Taurus, fill in the table below. Creating a table of information for yourself will help you connect to the essence of Taurus and understand its significant correlation with the Second House.

HOUSE NUMBER IN THE ZODIAC	SYMBOL	DATES	
		RULING PLANET	
STRENGTHS		WEAKNESSES	
DUALITY		ELEMENT	COLOR
MODALITY			

GEMINI ♊

KEY WORDS

communicator;
adaptable; quick-witted

**GEMINI
SEASON MANTRA**

Excitement and curiosity
are the driving forces.

Gemini is the third sign of the zodiac and therefore the natural ruler of the Third House. Gemini is the mutable air sign ruled by Mercury, the mythical messenger of the gods, symbolized by the twins and associated with the color yellow. These symbols are all clues to the meaning and energy of Gemini. Mutable signs are here to change throughout life and teach others how to do the same. The metaphor of the twins alludes to Gemini's ability to navigate duality and see multiple perspectives, while yellow is associated with joy and playfulness. These are core traits of Gemini, and your Sun in Gemini bestows upon you the gifts of a sharp intellect with a curious mind that thirsts for knowledge. Others may find you contradictory, but this is because few people have your ability to accept paradoxes and juggle multiple viewpoints.

During the time of year when the Sun makes its annual return through the jovial sign of Gemini, the pace of life seems to move at lightning speed. Social calendars are packed, your inbox is full, and it may feel like a struggle to focus on work when all you want to do is go out and play. This is when mighty Mercury is infusing its powers of enthusiastic communication into the collective while also recharging your energetic batteries, gearing you up for a new year of exploration and discovery. This is the perfect time to connect with others, be social, journal your thoughts, write that book, and be out in your community.

All about Gemini

Using the information you've learned about Gemini, fill in the table below. Creating a table of information for yourself will help you connect to the essence of Gemini and understand its significant correlation with the Third House.

HOUSE NUMBER IN THE ZODIAC	SYMBOL	DATES	
		RULING PLANET	
STRENGTHS		WEAKNESSES	
DUALITY		ELEMENT	COLOR
MODALITY			

CANCER ♋

JUNE 21–JULY 22

KEY WORDS

nurturing; emotional;
protective

**CANCER
SEASON MANTRA**

Check the vibes and
act accordingly.

Cancer is the fourth sign of the zodiac and therefore the natural ruler of the Fourth House. Cancer is the cardinal water sign ruled by the Moon, the mythical nurturing mother figure, symbolized by the crab and associated with the colors white or silver. These symbols are all clues to understanding the meaning and energy of Cancer. As I previously mentioned, cardinal energy correlates to initiating action, and while the sensitive crab moves sideways rather than forward, cautious of predators, it also carefully plots its moves in advance.

The Moon is connected to emotions and intuition, and this is one of your greatest gifts as a Cancer Sun. Your strong intuition and emotional range can be off-putting to those who are not as in touch with their own emotions. But don't let anyone tell you that you're too emotional! Others just may not understand your access to subtle psychic energies, ripples that can only be perceived by someone with your depth of feeling.

Remember how nostalgic you got at the end of each school year? Signing yearbooks and connecting with your classmates, reminiscing before summer vacation? This is some serious Cancer season energy, and when the Sun makes its annual trip through the sign of emotional introspection, the collective notices. We all realize we're already halfway through the year, and it is time to reflect back on how far we have come. This is when your Sun (and everyone else) is getting a megadose of the Moon's silvery reflection, bringing a time of turning inward and connecting with your intuition.

All about Cancer

Using the information you've learned about Cancer, fill in the table below. Creating a table of information for yourself will help you connect to the essence of Cancer and understand its significant correlation with the Fourth House.

HOUSE NUMBER IN THE ZODIAC	SYMBOL	DATES	
		RULING PLANET	
STRENGTHS		WEAKNESSES	
DUALITY		ELEMENT	COLOR
MODALITY			

LEO ♌

JULY 21–AUGUST 22

KEY WORDS

loyal; expressive; proud

**LEO
SEASON MANTRA**

Be the light just by
being yourself.

Leo is the fifth sign of the zodiac and therefore the natural ruler of the Fifth House. Leo is the fixed fire sign ruled by the Sun, the luminary center of our solar system, symbolized by the lion and associated with the colors gold and orange. The symbols will offer you clues to understanding the meaning and energy of Leo. Like other fixed signs, Leo is proud and stubborn yet generous and radiant like its ruling planet, the Sun. Unfortunately, Leo can sometimes forget they are not the center of the universe. Remember that the lion is a brave leader who takes the well-being of others into consideration when making decisions, rather than thinking only of themselves. Gold is the color of royalty and associated with luxury, and as a Leo Sun, you love the finer things in life. You're here to experience them, so don't hold back! While others may find your confidence undesirable, you should never dim your light for the sake of others' comfort.

Leo energy is bold, dramatic, and wants recognition. No matter where in the world you are, when the Sun moves into its favorite sign, the spirit of enthusiastic self-expression becomes contagious and we all get a healthy dose, urging us to be playful, creative, and to express our individuality. During this time when you are getting a cosmic refill of solar forces that will sustain you through the coming year, allow yourself to shine bright!

All about Leo

Using the information you've learned about Leo, fill in the table below. Creating a table of information for yourself will help you connect to the essence of Leo and understand its significant correlation with the Fifth House.

HOUSE NUMBER IN THE ZODIAC	SYMBOL	DATES	
		RULING PLANET	
STRENGTHS		WEAKNESSES	
DUALITY		ELEMENT	COLOR
MODALITY			

VIRGO ♍

**AUGUST 23–
SEPTEMBER 22**

KEY WORDS
organized;
analytical; helpful

**VIRGO
SEASON MANTRA**
The mind-body
connection paves the
way for success.

Virgo is the sixth sign of the zodiac and therefore the natural ruler of the Sixth House. Virgo is the mutable earth sign ruled by Mercury, the mythical messenger of the gods, symbolized by a maiden bearing wheat and associated with the colors green and brown. These symbols are clues to the meaning and energy of Virgo. The maiden is reminiscent of Virgo's purity and the wheat is its connection to the Earth and hard work, while the colors green and brown echo the relationship to the earth element and nature. Mutable signs are here to evolve and to teach us how to grow and change over time. Virgo Suns are blessed with the ability to adapt and advance through their strong bonds to both the earthly realm and their own physical bodies. Virgos are legendary perfectionists, and others may feel that your Mercurial mind has a tendency to get caught up in the details, preventing you from moving on and seeing the bigger picture. However, this ability to see the small details and strive for perfection is how you evolve and show others how to have patience and take their time with each task.

Remember back to your youth when the final days of summer vacation waned and the excitement of back-to-school shopping had you excited for new notebooks and binders, gathering supplies, and getting organized? This is major Virgo season energy! Only Virgo's earthly perfectionist tendencies could get children out of the swimming pool and excited for studying. The urge to organize and learn new things at this time of year appeals to the collective no matter what age, as the Sun makes its annual trip through practical Virgo. This is when you receive a boost of beneficial focus and direction to get back on track toward your goals.

All about Virgo

Using the information you've learned about Virgo, fill in the table below. Creating a table of information for yourself will help you connect to the essence of Virgo and understand its significant correlation with the Sixth House.

HOUSE NUMBER IN THE ZODIAC	SYMBOL	DATES	
		RULING PLANET	
STRENGTHS		WEAKNESSES	
DUALITY		ELEMENT	COLOR
MODALITY			

LIBRA ♎

**SEPTEMBER 23–
OCTOBER 22**

KEY WORDS

balanced; charming;
romantic

**LIBRA
SEASON MANTRA**

Speak up for your
needs in order to
achieve balance.

Libra is the seventh sign in the zodiac and therefore the natural ruler of the Seventh House. Libra is the cardinal air sign ruled by Venus, the mythical goddess of love and beauty, symbolized by the scales of justice and associated with the colors pink and blue. These symbols are all clues to the meaning and energy of Libra. Cardinal signs are here to initiate, yet the scales of Libra show the constant seeking of balance, which can lead to a passive-aggressive nature rather than taking a direct approach like other cardinal signs. As a Libra Sun, you are ruled by gentle Venus, gifting you with heaps of charm and a soft power of persuasion. Others may see your passivity as indecisive, but it may just be challenging for them to understand you are merely weighing all options in search of the most harmonious result.

When the Sun makes its annual tour of lovely Libra, the entire collective experiences a boost of romantic Venus's energy. Often referred to as "cuffing season," Libra loves to flirt, as this amorous air sign has a way with words and is easily charmed by the stylish sentiments of others. This is also a time of seeking balance and harmony, as the collective engages in both inner and outer work in all areas of life. While the Sun is in the sign of partnership, you are getting a boost of relational energy that will help you find your own voice and solidify your place as an individual within your significant relationships.

All about Libra

Using the information you've learned about Libra, fill in the table below. Creating a table of information for yourself will help you connect to the essence of Libra and understand its significant correlation with the Seventh House.

HOUSE NUMBER IN THE ZODIAC	SYMBOL	DATES	
		RULING PLANET	
STRENGTHS		WEAKNESSES	
DUALITY		ELEMENT	COLOR
MODALITY			

SCORPIO ♏

OCTOBER 23–
NOVEMBER 21

KEY WORDS
intense; self-protective;
determined

**SCORPIO
SEASON MANTRA**
Letting go clears the
path for new beginnings.

Scorpio is the eighth sign of the zodiac and therefore the natural ruler of the Eighth House. Scorpio is the fixed water sign ruled classically by Mars and more recently by Pluto, the mythical god of war and lord of the underworld, symbolized by the scorpion, and associated with the colors red and black. These symbols will give you clues to the meaning and energy of Scorpio. Before Pluto was discovered, Scorpio was considered to be ruled by Mars, however the nature of Scorpio is more complex than the red planet alone can offer. The transformative tale of the Scorpion becoming a hawk and later a phoenix rising from the ashes is more befitting of your potent energy. Others may find your constant state of being remade through massive personal change too intense, however, this is where your true power lies, within the delicate dance of control and surrender. Not everyone was built to walk through fire and come out the other side transformed.

Each year when the Sun moves through the dark waters of Scorpio, we witness the changing landscape as the trees turn from green to golden yellows, vibrant oranges and reds, and finally to brown as they shed their protective coverings, leaving them vulnerable and exposed. This is when the collective experiences our own personal shedding and deep introspection, and you get a potent dose of regenerative energy that will assist you in shedding the things that no longer serve you in order to make space for what's to come in the following year.

All about Scorpio

Using the information you've learned about Scorpio, fill in the table below. Creating a table of information for yourself will help you connect to the essence of Scorpio and understand its significant correlation with the Eighth House.

HOUSE NUMBER IN THE ZODIAC	SYMBOL	DATES
		RULING PLANET
STRENGTHS		WEAKNESSES
DUALITY		ELEMENT	COLOR
MODALITY			

SAGITTARIUS ♐

**NOVEMBER 22–
DECEMBER 21**

KEY WORDS
adventurous; sarcastic;
truth-seeking

**SAGITTARIUS
SEASON MANTRA**
Grow through what
you go through.

Sagittarius is the ninth sign of the zodiac and therefore the natural ruler of the Ninth House. Sagittarius is the mutable fire sign ruled by Jupiter, the mythical god of the gods, symbolized by the archer's bow and arrow and associated with the color purple. These symbols are clues to the meaning and energy of Sagittarius, as mutable energy is here to evolve and teach us how to grow and change. Sagittarians show how to seek truth by launching themselves fearlessly into new situations; taking risks and pushing your luck excites you, and often you can't lose! When you do run into a roadblock or challenge, you find it to be an enriching personal-growth experience rather than a failure—an optimism that some may see as reckless. You easily let things roll off your back without strong emotional attachment.

The hallmark energy of Sagittarius season is the bustling holiday season, filled with family gatherings and frenetic end-of-year planning. Ever notice how your holiday gatherings are fraught with bickering? This is major Sagittarius energy, unafraid to speak the truth, taking all that has been unsaid and dragging it out into the light to be dealt with. The collective is experiencing the need for freedom of expression and, frankly, a little brisk-paced drama. Your natural enthusiasm is getting a boost during this time, lighting your candle at both ends to move you into the upcoming year at lightning speed.

All about Sagittarius

Using the information you've learned about Sagittarius, fill in the table below. Creating a table of information for yourself will help you connect to the essence of Sagittarius and understand its significant correlation with the Ninth House.

HOUSE NUMBER IN THE ZODIAC	SYMBOL	DATES
		RULING PLANET
STRENGTHS		WEAKNESSES
DUALITY	ELEMENT	COLOR
MODALITY		

CAPRICORN ♑

DECEMBER 22–
JANUARY 20

KEY WORDS
focused; dedicated;
unrelenting

**CAPRICORN
SEASON MANTRA**
Amazing things come to
those who persist.

Capricorn is the tenth sign of the zodiac and therefore the natural ruler of the Tenth House. Capricorn is the cardinal earth sign ruled by Saturn, the mythical ruler of time, symbolized by the sea goat and associated with the colors gray and brown. These symbols are all clues to the meaning and energy of Capricorn. The colors gray and brown link Capricorn to both land and sea, and Saturn's rule bestows the gifts of patience, focus, determination, and unparalleled ambition. Cardinal signs are initiators, and the sea goat is fiercely determined to navigate the emotional as well as material realm. While you may not be comfortable expressing your feelings, you have a rich and intense emotional world and are discerning about the people with whom you share yourself. Others may see you as cold or work-obsessed; however, you are extremely loving, generous, and dedicated to those you care about.

Capricorn energy is the driving force that propels the collective into the new year, getting everyone back on track by recommitting to our personal goals with a renewed energy to achieve them. When the Sun makes its annual transit through ambitious Capricorn, it's a great time to form new habits, recommit to your goals, and take action on things you've been putting off. This is when you are personally getting a megadose of Saturn's no-nonsense focus to take massive action on your loftiest goals. You know you won't accomplish everything in one month, so you're playing the long game and delighting in every step.

All about Capricorn

Using the information you've learned about Capricorn, fill in the table below. Creating a table of information for yourself will help you connect to the essence of Capricorn and understand its significant correlation with the Tenth House.

HOUSE NUMBER IN THE ZODIAC	SYMBOL	DATES	
		RULING PLANET	
STRENGTHS		WEAKNESSES	
DUALITY		ELEMENT	COLOR
MODALITY			

AQUARIUS ≋

KEY WORDS

friendship focused; innovative; rebellious

AQUARIUS SEASON MANTRA

You don't have to fit in to belong.

Aquarius is the eleventh sign of the zodiac and therefore the natural ruler of the Eleventh House. Aquarius is the fixed air sign ruled classically by Saturn and its modern ruler Uranus, mythical ruler of time and god of the sky, symbolized by the Water Bearer, and associated with the color blue. These symbols are all clues to the meaning and energy of Aquarius. Before Uranus was discovered, Aquarius was ruled by Saturn; however, the erratic and unpredictable nature of Aquarius wasn't enough for Saturn alone to contain. Fixed signs are known for their stubborn, immovable nature, and Aquarius can be quite attached to their opinions and ideas while simultaneously detached from the physical world. Others may find your contrarian behavior shocking or rebellious; however, not everyone can see your vision or hold the same futuristic outlook, preferring tangible evidence to innovative theory. Your ability to think new ideas into existence helps guide others off the path of resistance and into a future that benefits the group rather than merely the individual.

The Sun makes its annual transit through innovative Aquarius at the beginning of each new year, bringing new ideas to be carried out over the coming months. The collective is feeling galvanized to make change, even if it remains in the conceptual stages. While the Sun is in Aquarius, take the opportunity to write down any ideas or insights that come to you, join a new group or club, get involved in a social cause, and don't be afraid to stand out by expressing your quirks. You are getting a cosmic refresh in your social groups as well as your hopes and dreams for the future. Don't hold back from sharing your unique perspective.

All about Aquarius

Using the information you've learned about Aquarius, fill in the table below. Creating a table of information for yourself will help you connect to the essence of Aquarius and understand its significant correlation with the Eleventh House.

HOUSE NUMBER IN THE ZODIAC	SYMBOL	DATES	
		RULING PLANET	
STRENGTHS		WEAKNESSES	
DUALITY		ELEMENT	COLOR
MODALITY			

PISCES ♓

KEY WORDS

dreamy; intuitive;
empathetic

**PISCES
SEASON MANTRA**

The glass may be half
full or half empty; how
you view it is always
a choice.

Pisces is the twelfth and final sign of the zodiac, therefore it is the natural ruler of the Twelfth House. Pisces is the mutable water sign ruled classically by Jupiter and its modern ruler Neptune, mythical god of the sea, symbolized by two fish swimming in opposing directions and associated with the color pale green. These symbols will offer you clues to the meaning and energy of Pisces. Mutable signs are here to evolve and change over time and teach the rest of us to do the same, while the fish swimming in opposite directions further illustrate a constant state of emotional flux as well as depth of feeling and intuition. Fish lack protective armor like the other water signs, and bearing their vulnerable scales without pretense lends itself to the immense feelings of compassion and empathy of which they are capable. While others may perceive you as dreamy and otherworldly, they may not understand your deep connection to the subtle realms beyond visual perception. Your intuition is your internal GPS, so trust its accuracy and allow it to guide you through life.

As the final house of the zodiac, Pisces energy is at peace with endings, and at the time of year when the Sun is transiting through this emotional sign, the collective is experiencing the end of winter in the Northern Hemisphere. The final frosts that come before the return of spring have us daydreaming about the magical possibilities a new season will bring. While the Sun is in sensitive Pisces, it's a great time to tie up loose ends, wrap up existing projects, make a vision board for what comes next, and focus on romantic gestures for your special someone (and especially yourself). You are getting a cosmic reset in your emotional world, as well as a hefty dose of Neptune's idealism for the upcoming year.

All about Pisces

Using the information you've learned about Pisces, fill in the table below. Creating a table of information for yourself will help you connect to the essence of Pisces and understand its significant correlation with the Twelfth House.

HOUSE NUMBER IN THE ZODIAC	SYMBOL	DATES	
		RULING PLANET	
STRENGTHS		WEAKNESSES	
DUALITY		ELEMENT	COLOR
MODALITY			

Working with My Birth Chart: My Sun Sign

1. Locate the symbol for Sun in your chart and see which house your Sun falls in.

2. My Sun is in ....in the .... House, meaning the brightest part of my chart and my personality is here to focus on the .... area of life.

3. What strong attributes do you as a .... sign already possess in this area? ....

4. My sign is expressed as .... in modality, which means ....

5. It is characterized as .... in duality, which can be interpreted as ....

6. What characteristics of your Sun sign or the house in which your Sun resides are you curious about cultivating?
....
....

7. Take a moment to compare your sign's element and the element of the natural ruler of the house. For example, are you a fire sign in an Earth house? How do you think that affects your personality?
....
....

REFLECTION

Which attributes associated with your Sun sign resonate with your core personality and which ones seem off base? This information will come in handy as you learn more about your Moon sign and inner planets in the following chapters.
....
....

NOTES

FOUR

Meeting the Moon Signs

· · · · · · · · · · · · · · · · · · · ·

NOW YOU KNOW that the Sun in your birth chart represents your core personality and can help you clarify what you are meant to do in this lifetime. The Moon is the second luminary in our solar system and nearly as important as the Sun in terms of its influence on your chart. As the Moon revolves around the Earth and is our closest celestial body, it exerts control over the oceans' tides. Its cyclical phases remind us of our connection to the water in our bodies, as well as the waxing and waning of our own emotions. This means that the Moon's role in our birth charts is to influence our private selves, the aspects of our identities that we only show to people with whom we feel a sense of safety and comfort (i.e., family, romantic partners, and close friends).

The Moon also represents your psyche and emotional nature. The house and sign in which it falls show you what you need to feel emotionally secure and how you self-soothe. It also offers insight into your relationship with your mother (as well as the ways you mother yourself). The element of your Moon sign is extremely important to understanding yourself on a deeper psychological level. For instance, people with earth Moons are grounded, practical, and crave stability to feel safe, while those with fire Moons express themselves passionately and need an outlet for their fiery emotions. Air Moons need communication and mental stimulation to satisfy them emotionally, and water Moons crave intimacy and depth of feeling.

MOON IN ARIES

KEY WORDS: individualist; hot temper; need for freedom

The Moon in Aries is ruled by fiery, feisty Mars. This placement gives you a need for individual expression, meaning you loathe being told what to do and where to be. Aries Moons need plenty of freedom to explore, seeking out excitement and adventure. In order to feel emotionally secure, you need to take charge of your inner world and have plenty of opportunities to take action toward whatever strikes your fancy. Fire Moons in general are passionate and highly excitable. With Mars as your Moon's ruler you may find yourself quick to react or become infamous for your quick temper. Fortunately, fire burns hot but only momentarily; once a strong feeling passes, you rarely hang on to it. Giving yourself permission to express your emotions and taking some time to journal about what triggers these eruptions will help you understand yourself on a deeper level.

At your best, you are incredibly passionate, confident, and fearless. You are a natural leader and risk-taker, paving the way for others to step out of their comfort zones and dive into the action.

MOON IN TAURUS

KEY WORDS: decadent; slow-paced; sensual

The Moon in Taurus is ruled by indulgent, romantic Venus. This placement gives you a need for decadence, sensuality, and experiencing life's pleasures at your own pace, meaning you love when others defer to your tastes when choosing restaurants or making plans. Taurus Moons need to feel in control of their surroundings, opting for places that are beautiful and inspiring, helping them to feel emotionally secure. Earth Moons in general detest being rushed and will only move at their own pace. Taurus, being one of the slowest moving signs, delights in having all the time in the world. Savoring every delicious moment brings you a sense of peace, even if it frustrates your loved ones. With Venus as your Moon's ruler, you may find yourself stubbornly focused on your own sense of comfort rather than compromising with the people in your life.

At your best, you are devoted, romantic, and have impeccable taste, making you a favorite companion for any occasion.

MOON IN GEMINI

KEY WORDS: intellectualizing; talkative; restless

The Moon in Gemini is ruled by quick-witted Mercury. This placement gives you a need for intellectual stimulation, communication, and processing your feelings mentally before you feel them emotionally. Your mind is constantly on the move, seeking out information and answers, which may leave you feeling restless. Gemini Moons feel secure when they have all the facts and are able to communicate their experiences by verbally processing them with trusted friends or partners or through the written word via practices like journaling. Air Moons in general process their emotional world through an intellectual lens, and Gemini is able to ingest information at an incredibly fast pace. With Mercury as your Moon's ruler, you may find yourself enthralled with experiences and relationships that offer you a buffet of new information to devour, only to find yourself bored and looking for the next thing once you've seen all there is to see.

At your best, you are fun to be around, a great conversationalist, and always up for an adventure, making you popular among your social circles.

MOON IN CANCER

KEY WORDS: moody; emotional; nurturing

The Moon in Cancer is ruled by the Moon itself, making this one of the most intuitive, nurturing, and often emotionally erratic placements for the Moon to occupy. With your Moon in its natural domicile, anything that supports emotional security and a feeling of safety is essential to your sense of well-being. You feel things deeply, and with this highly empathic placement, you have the ability to feel the emotions of others around you. This leads to a need for plenty of time alone to process your feelings and cleanse yourself of the energetic residue following heavy interactions. Water Moons in general are incredibly intuitive and nurturing, as they can sense the energy of any situation and have an innate understanding of the underlying subtext, even when others are reluctant to share their feelings. Unfortunately, Cancer Moons can internalize not only their own emotions but also the energy they absorb from others, leading them to feel weighed down if they do not allow themselves to release these emotions through talking about their feelings or having a good cry.

At your best, you are psychic, compassionate, and deeply loving, making you a sought-after source of emotional support.

MOON IN LEO

KEY WORDS: dramatic; charismatic; attention-seeking

The Moon in Leo is ruled by the Sun, giving this placement a double dose of illumination. With the brightest light in the solar system ruling *la luna*, what is typically a private placement becomes public, since you are inclined to share your emotions and the details of your inner life. Recognition and validation of your feelings and experiences are vital to your sense of security. Rather than processing your feelings privately, you prefer to share your inner world with others. Fire Moons in general have a dramatic sense of self-expression, which may include a quick temper or highly charged emotional responses (including excitement and enthusiasm). With the Sun as your Moon's ruler, creative self-expression is an essential part of self-soothing for you. Leo Moons love the spotlight in any capacity, demanding attention and recognition almost constantly. Visibility is a good thing for you, as it helps you process your emotional landscape and gain a better understanding of yourself and your psychological needs.

At your best, you are vivacious, charismatic, and expressive, making you a force to be reckoned with and an inspiration to those around you.

MOON IN VIRGO

KEY WORDS: helpful; perfectionist; pragmatic

The Moon in Virgo is ruled by analytical Mercury, giving this placement a restless mind. So restless that it often needs a physical outlet to counterbalance the immense mental activity it experiences. Your Moon in Virgo is service-oriented and derives emotional satisfaction by being helpful and valuable to others. Much like Gemini Moons, Virgo Moons tend to process their emotions through an intellectual lens before feeling them in their bodies. With Mercury as your Moon's ruler, your mind is constantly taking in information, scanning it, and looking for ways to optimize your experiences, especially when those experiences can benefit others. Earth Moons in general are grounded, practical, and methodical when it comes to taking action and making decisions. Putting yourself in risky situations is highly stressful for you. You prefer to analyze your options and come up with a sensible strategy before diving into new situations. Experiencing the world at your own pace gives you a sense of control and stability that allows you to push yourself past your limitations, to grow and evolve.

At your best, you are a supportive, accommodating problem-solver, making you indispensable to your loved ones.

MOON IN LIBRA

KEY WORDS: agreeable; harmonious; partner-focused

The Moon in Libra is ruled by charming, romantic Venus. This placement gives you a need for harmony and diplomacy in your relationships to feel an overall sense of safety and security. Nothing stresses you out more than arguments, rudeness, or disagreements that can't be easily resolved. Your Moon in Libra can also make you get stuck weighing the pros and cons of every situation, leading to indecisiveness that may irritate others. Considering all possibilities is actually a great source of emotional fulfillment for you, though, as it allows you to tap into your gift for inner analysis. Have patience with yourself when you feel rushed by others to make a decision, and enjoy your process. Air signs in general are stimulated by mental activity and communication. You are a romantic at your core, and your Venusian-ruled Libra Moon loves beautiful words, be they poetry, prose, love letters, or just great conversation. Having something or someone to romanticize is an essential part of your interior landscape that fuels your creativity.

At your best, you are flirty, charming, and a lover of beauty, making you an easy choice for anyone to want to be around.

MOON IN SCORPIO

KEY WORDS: private; intense; secretive

The Moon in Scorpio is ruled by aggressive Mars and intensely transformative Pluto. This placement gives you a deep need for intimacy, privacy, and loyalty to feel emotional security. Feeling safe is a constant struggle for Scorpio Moons, since you rarely feel like you can trust anyone besides yourself. This also makes it a challenge for you to open up to others and show your soft vulnerability. When you choose to do so, opening yourself up to the possibility of experiencing pain is the only true path to the intimacy you so desire. Water Moons in general are incredibly intuitive and able to sense the underlying motivations and energy of those around them. Unfortunately, this can lead to mistrust and shutting down emotionally in order to feel protected. Your Plutonian-ruled Moon is here to help you transcend your complex emotions rather than hiding them away. Journaling or talk therapy can be a healthy way to excavate your intense feelings so you can better understand yourself as you navigate your complex inner world.

At your best, you are loyal, intuitive, and deeply romantic, which makes you an ideal long-term partner for those who are worthy of your love.

MOON IN SAGITTARIUS

KEY WORDS: adventurous; freedom-loving; optimistic

The Moon in Sagittarius is ruled by expansive Jupiter. This placement gives you a need for adventure, freedom, and a thirst for learning. Feeling safe and secure happens when you have the opportunity to grow and expand your worldview. You're optimistic and lighthearted, but you take your inner need for the truth very seriously. You value honesty and "tell it like it is" without taking other's reactions to your truth-bombs personally. Fire Moons in general are expressive, passionate, and creative, and your Moon in Sagittarius gifts you with an innate sense of wonder for novel experiences. You thrive in situations where you are learning or trying new things. Your need for fresh perspectives and newness can make it challenging for you to commit to one person or career path, and that isn't a bad thing. You are here to experience a myriad of relationships and lifestyles so you can learn about yourself and the world around you. Trying to force yourself into any particular role or path would be detrimental to your development.

At your best, you are friendly, wise, and exciting to be around, making you the ultimate companion to others as they broaden their horizons.

MOON IN CAPRICORN

KEY WORDS: serious; practical; productive

The Moon in Capricorn is ruled by restrictive task-master Saturn. This placement gives a somber, serious nature that thrives on structure and self-discipline to feel safe and secure. This doesn't mean you are all work and no play; you just value completing your tasks before you relax and enjoy leisure activities. Despite the stoic nature of the Moon in Capricorn, you are actually very sensitive, although you may choose not to let others know this about you. Remember, it's healthy for you to open up and show your emotions. Accessing your vulnerability is key to helping you establish intimacy and connection within your close relationships. Earth Moons in general are practical, grounded, and take their time, preferring not to rush situations. Taking your time and creating a strategy before acting help you feel a sense of control and stability that is essential to your sense of well-being.

At your best, you are responsible, driven, and a grounding force for yourself and everyone around you, making you a source of inspiration and stability for the people who care about you.

MOON IN AQUARIUS

KEY WORDS: detached; observant; independent

The Moon in Aquarius is ruled by restrictive Saturn and unpredictable Uranus, giving you the characteristics of both emotional detachment and freedom-loving independence. This means you need to have plenty of space to observe and assimilate the world around you in order to feel a sense of security. Your keen observational skills allow you to see things in people that others might overlook, meaning you enjoy quirky, offbeat traits that often go unnoticed or uncelebrated.

Air Moons in general thrive on the exchange of information, communication, and mental stimulation, so your Moon in Aquarius means you crave plenty of uninterrupted privacy to pour over details and assimilate all the data you receive. While others may perceive you as cold or detached from your emotions, this is just your way of processing your feelings through an intellectual lens. In fact, you care deeply for the people in your life as well as the humanitarian causes that affect the world at large.

At your best, you are an inquisitive observer of the world with an eye for the unconventional, making you a surprise force to be reckoned with when you share your impressions with others.

MOON IN PISCES

KEY WORDS: sensitive; intuitive; empathetic

The Moon in Pisces is ruled by spiritual, expansive Jupiter and dreamy, nebulous Neptune. Due to the highly intuitive nature of Pisces, this placement is prone to deep, empathic feelings that can cause you to identify too heavily with the suffering of others and the collective pain of the planet. Having your Moon in Pisces asks you to find ways to protect yourself from taking on the heavy energies of others so you can utilize your intuitive gifts in productive ways. Water Moons in general operate on instinct, as they have natural psychic abilities that come in the form of feelings that cannot be explained rationally. This inner knowing is your guide to feeling secure in the world. Pay attention to your gut when a space, situation, or person feels off; also heed your instincts when you feel safe and cared for. Your Pisces Moon bestows you with vivid dreams that can be channeled through media such as music, art, and poetry, which will lead to emotional fulfillment. Rather than escaping reality, create your own by tapping into this creativity.

At your best, you are kind, caring, understanding, and a wonderful source of support for those around you, making you a beloved friend in times of need.

Working with My Birth Chart: My Moon Sign

1. Look at your birth chart and find the Moon glyph: ☽.

2. My Moon is in ...., which gives me the characteristics of ....

3. My sign is expressed as .... in modality, which means ....

4. It is characterized as .... in duality, which can be interpreted as ....

5. What house is your Moon sign in? ....

6. List the characteristics of the natural ruler of the house your Moon sign falls in and compare them
    to the characteristics of your Moon sign. ....
    ....
    ....

7. How do you think having your Moon in the .... House affects your personality and
    emotional landscape? ....
    ....
    ....

REFLECTION

Based on what you now know about your Moon sign, what are three key things that help you feel
emotionally secure?

....

....

....

....

....

NOTES

....
....
....
....
....
....
....
....
....
....
....
....
....
....
....
....
....
....
....
....
....
....
....
....
....

FIVE

Puzzling Out the Ascendant Signs

· · · · · · · · · · · · · · · · · · · ·

GIVEN HOW ASTROLOGY is presented in the mainstream, you may have assumed your Sun sign was the most important piece of your chart, and understandably so! Now you've learned that your Moon sign adds even more depth, and you're about to find out how your Ascendant sign has a profound impact on the themes of your life.

Also known as your "rising sign," your Ascendant sign is calculated using your birth time to determine which sign was on the eastern horizon at the exact moment of your birth. This element of your chart describes your outermost layer of identity: how people perceive you and the first impression you make on others. This explains why, when we first meet someone, we introduce ourselves as our Ascendant, and only once we feel comfortable and safe can we begin to show our Sun and eventually our Moon sign. For example, those with a Libra rising are ruled by Venus and will have Venusian qualities such as charm, grace, and a sensual nature about them, while a Gemini rising, which is ruled by Mercury, will have the Mercurial qualities of mental agility and quick wit. Your Ascendant sign is a natural resource to aid your Sun sign in carrying out the unique assignments it has for you in this lifetime.

ARIES ASCENDANT

KEY WORDS: confident; enthusiastic

The Aries Ascendant is the natural ruler of the First House and is ruled by fiery, assertive Mars. This placement gives you natural leadership abilities along with a brave, independent spirit that seeks opportunities to take risks and show off your skills and abilities. You may come off as intimidating to some, since your ruling planet is known as the god of war. With Mars as your chart ruler, you don't shy away from an argument or a challenge. Aries is categorized as a daytime sign, otherwise known as diurnal. This means that your Aries rising expresses itself as outwardly and extroverted, rather than nighttime signs that express themselves emotionally and more introverted. With Aries as your Ascendant sign, you enjoy being the center of attention or at the very least receiving recognition for your efforts. The first impression you give others is one of a confident, assertive, and enthusiastic nature, so people perceive you as being more than capable of handling any task and ready for any challenge.

TAURUS ASCENDANT

KEY WORDS: relaxed; self-assured

The Taurus Ascendant is ruled by charming, beautiful Venus. With Venus as your chart ruler, you seek harmonious relationships, beautiful surroundings, and are equipped with a natural sense of who you are and where you are going. The Taurus Ascendant gives you all of the Venusian qualities of grace, self-assurance, and sensuality without the same stubbornness of a Taurus Sun. Taurus is categorized as a nighttime sign, otherwise known as nocturnal. This means that your Taurus rising expresses itself emotionally and introverted, rather than daytime, or diurnal, signs that express themselves outwardly and more extroverted. People perceive you as relaxed and comfortable in your own skin, emotionally steady, and easy to be around. It may take you some time to open up to others and let them get to know you, but once you feel solid in the relationship, you are a wonderful friend and partner who is dependable and can always be counted on.

GEMINI ASCENDANT

KEY WORDS: bright; talkative

The Gemini Ascendant is ruled by chatty, inquisitive Mercury. With the messenger of the gods as your ruling planet, this placement gives you the gift of gab and a thirst for mental stimulation, as well as making you the unofficial social butterfly of the zodiac. Having Mercury as your chart ruler places communication at the heart of all that you do, aiding your Sun sign in making important connections to help guide you through the unique experiences you'll have in this lifetime (which may include writing, public speaking, or communication in general). Gemini is categorized as a daytime sign, otherwise known as diurnal. This means that your Gemini rising expresses itself outwardly and extroverted, rather than nighttime signs that express themselves emotionally and more introverted. People perceive you as bright, vivacious, and naturally curious about others, making you an excellent conversationalist who helps them feel at ease expressing themselves.

CANCER ASCENDANT

KEY WORDS: nurturing; sweet

The Cancer Ascendant is ruled by the intuitive, caring Moon. With *la luna* as your ruling planet, this placement gives you substantial emotional intelligence that is meant to fluctuate as you surrender to your feelings. Having the Moon as your chart ruler lends you the gifts of strong intuition and a deeply caring nature to aid your Sun sign by guiding it through the unique experiences you'll have during this lifetime. Cancer is categorized as a nighttime sign, otherwise known as nocturnal. This means that your Cancer rising expresses itself emotionally and introverted, rather than daytime, or diurnal, signs that express themselves outwardly and more extroverted. People perceive you as caring, sweet, and compassionate and may attach themselves to you as they seek the comforts of a maternal figure (regardless of your gender identity). While it feels good to feel needed, maintaining healthy boundaries within your relationships empowers those around you to care for themselves.

LEO ASCENDANT

KEY WORDS: dramatic; charismatic

The Leo Ascendant is ruled by our larger-than-life Sun, giving this placement a bold, dramatic presence that refuses to be ignored. Even if you have an introverted Sun or Moon sign, having the Sun as your ruling planet gifts you a golden sparkle that others cannot help but notice. Leo risings have a natural warmth that makes them fun to be around, especially when they shine their light out onto others, becoming the best cheerleader one could ask for. With the Sun as your chart ruler, your Sun sign receives the brightest luminary in the galaxy to shine upon you as you navigate the unique experiences you're meant to encounter in this lifetime. Leo is categorized as a daytime sign, otherwise known as diurnal. This means that your Leo rising expresses itself outwardly and extroverted, rather than nighttime signs that express themselves emotionally and more introverted. People perceive you as supportive and enthusiastic, and you bring a refreshing dose of pure positive energy to every gathering.

VIRGO ASCENDANT

KEY WORDS: intelligent; organized

The Virgo Ascendant is ruled by inquisitive, intelligent Mercury, giving this placement an inherent curiosity and proclivity for intellectual stimulation. Perfectionist tendencies are a hallmark of all Virgo placements, as you crave order and seek the most efficient strategies for development and executing tasks. With Mercury as your ruling planet, it is your nature to question everything you encounter, including yourself, which can lead to self-critical tendencies. You enjoy being of service to others, and with having Mercury as your chart ruler, you're likely to be gifted at communication. This gift will assist your Sun sign in making any necessary connections as you navigate the unique experiences you are meant to have in this lifetime. Virgo is categorized as a nighttime sign, otherwise known as nocturnal. This means that your Virgo rising expresses itself emotionally and introverted, rather than daytime, or diurnal, signs that express themselves outwardly and more extroverted. People perceive you as helpful, intelligent, and detail-oriented, and they will seek out your help in various ways, which gives you a tremendous sense of personal satisfaction.

LIBRA ASCENDANT

KEY WORDS: charming; agreeable

The Libra Ascendant is ruled by lovely, romantic Venus, giving this placement the benefits of an attractive personality, innate sophistication, and charm. Having Venus as your ruling planet, you tend to present yourself as agreeable and pleasant, making sure to always put your best foot forward, especially in situations where you feel uncomfortable. You have a natural tendency to tune in to the energy of others and are able to mirror them in ways that make them instantly comfortable around you. With sophisticated Venus as your chart ruler, your aesthetic gifts and refined social graces assist your Sun sign in navigating the unique relationships and experiences you're meant to have in this lifetime. Libra is categorized as a daytime sign, otherwise known as diurnal. This means that your Libra rising expresses itself outwardly and extroverted, rather than nighttime signs that express themselves emotionally and more introverted. People perceive you as alluring, sociable, and generally approachable, which helps you feel at ease and in control when traversing new environments.

SCORPIO ASCENDANT

KEY WORDS: mysterious; powerful

The Scorpio Ascendant is ruled by both aggressive Mars and powerful Pluto, giving this placement a quiet intensity that can come across as intimidating and mysterious. Your ruling planets bestow you with a magnetic sexual presence even when you're not trying to be overtly sexy. With both Mars and Pluto as your chart rulers, you have access to Pluto's deeply transformative energies combined with the initiative capabilities of Mars, a combination that helps your Sun sign to maximize the incredible and unique metamorphosis you are here to experience in this lifetime. Scorpio is categorized as a nighttime sign, otherwise known as nocturnal. This means that your Scorpio rising expresses itself emotionally and introverted, rather than daytime, or diurnal, signs that express themselves outwardly and more extroverted. People experience you as somewhat polarizing, since your magnetic aura of power, control, surrender, and rebirth affects everyone you encounter. You are here to be a catalyst for yourself and others, leading them to change just by being yourself.

SAGITTARIUS ASCENDANT

KEY WORDS: optimistic; lucky

The Sagittarius Ascendant is ruled by expansive, optimistic Jupiter, giving this placement a natural sense of wonder and enthusiasm. You are constantly seeking adventure, eager to taste all that life has to offer, open to learning about yourself and the world around you. Having Jupiter as your ruling planet gifts you with a huge appetite for experience, preferring to learn by leaping before you look. With Jupiter as your chart ruler, you tend to always land on your feet, absorbing any lessons while easily letting go of the emotions attached to them. This helps your Sun sign guide you through the unique experiences you are meant to have in this lifetime. Sagittarius is categorized as a daytime sign, otherwise known as diurnal. This means that your Sagittarius rising expresses itself outwardly and extroverted, rather than nighttime signs that express themselves emotionally and more introverted. People see you as upbeat, friendly, and lucky. No matter what life throws at you, you always make the most of it and learn something new about yourself and the world.

CAPRICORN ASCENDANT

KEY WORDS: driven; earnest

The Capricorn Ascendant is ruled by serious, task-oriented Saturn, which gives this placement a natural sense of duty and responsibility to goals and particularly careers. You are incredibly ambitious and don't spend a lot of time on people and projects that aren't supportive of your enterprising objectives. With Saturn as your ruling planet, you understand that success takes time. You value each step it takes to reach your goals and continue to take those steps without hesitation. Having Saturn as your chart ruler gives you the maturity to take your life seriously, even from a young age, leading you to feel responsible for others. While that can feel burdensome, it is a gift to your Sun sign, helping you reach incredible heights via the unique experiences you are meant to have in this lifetime. Capricorn is categorized as a nighttime sign, otherwise known as nocturnal. This just means that your Capricorn rising expresses itself emotionally and introverted, rather than daytime, or diurnal, signs that express themselves outwardly and more extroverted. People perceive you as driven and in control of your destiny, looking up to you as an example and inspiration.

AQUARIUS ASCENDANT

KEY WORDS: quirky; social-justice minded

The Aquarius Ascendant is ruled by both restrictive Saturn and unpredictable Uranus, giving this placement a unique blend of Uranus's revolutionary rebelliousness and the task-orientation of Saturn that will help you stick to your plans and achieve your goals. Having Saturn and Uranus as your ruling planets makes you uncategorizable to others, and that's just how you like it. Your chart rulers make you a natural catalyst for change, both in yourself and within society, by emphasizing your futuristic outlook and pioneering social-justice causes. Aquarius is categorized as a daytime sign, otherwise known as diurnal. This means that your Aquarius rising expresses itself outwardly and extroverted, rather than nighttime signs that express themselves emotionally and more introverted. People perceive you as edgy, eccentric, and unconventional in your approach from your lifestyle to your political views. Never censor yourself—your ideas are meant to be shared, no matter how unorthodox they may seem.

PISCES ASCENDANT

KEY WORDS: dreamy; alluring

The Pisces Ascendant is ruled by both expansive, spiritual Jupiter and imaginative, nebulous Neptune, giving this placement an air of gentle sensitivity. You're likely to be highly intuitive and somewhat detached from the physical world, preferring to commune with the cosmos. With Jupiter and Neptune as your ruling planets, you have the gift of humanitarian passion that makes you an empathetic, natural caregiver who loves helping others in need. Your Jupiter and Neptune chart rulers are here to enlist your intuitive powers to guide your Sun sign through the unique experiences you'll experience in this lifetime. Pisces is categorized as a nighttime sign, otherwise known as nocturnal. This may sound complicated, but it just means that your Pisces rising expresses itself emotionally and introverted, rather than daytime, or diurnal, signs that express themselves outwardly and more extroverted. People perceive you as alluring and somewhat otherworldly and are therefore naturally drawn to you. You benefit from following your intuition to see people and situations more clearly.

Working with My Birth Chart: My Ascendant

1. My Sun is in the .... House, in the sign of ....
    at .... degrees.

2. My Moon is in the .... House, in the sign of ....
    at .... degrees.

3. My Ascendant sign is in .... at .... degrees, and
    .... is my chart ruler.

REFLECTION

Knowing that your Ascendant sign is ruled by a specific planet or planets and that they are considered your chart ruler, how do you think that energy affects how you move through the world? How do you feel about how your Ascendant sign works in tandem with your Sun sign?

....

....

....

....

....

....

....

....

....

....

....

....

....

NOTES

SIX

Investigating the Inner Planets

....

EXPLORING YOUR BIRTH chart is like getting to know a person. You start on the surface, discovering the traits and aspects of them that are the most obvious, and gradually dig deeper to see more and more of their true identity. Except in this case, you're actually getting to know yourself! And now that you've learned all about our Big Three—your Sun, Moon, and Ascendant—you are ready to meet and learn about the rest of the celestial bodies.

You now know that your birth chart shows each planet falling in a particular house and sign. The planets that are closest to the Sun—Mercury, Venus, and Mars—are known as inner planets or personal planets. They've earned this catchy nickname because of their proximity to the Sun and the speed at which they travel around the ecliptic. Both of these factors give them a ton of influence on your personality. Since the inner planets move more quickly through the zodiac signs, they influence the elements of your daily life. Compatibility between two people (romantic or otherwise) is determined mainly by looking at inner planets. Because they impact your day-to-day needs, behaviors, and patterns, they give clues about who'll align and who'll clash with that daily version of you!

Mercury, Venus, and Mars each have their own specific energy and play a vital role in helping shape who you are and how you interact with the world around you.

MERCURY ☿

KEY WORDS: communication; intellect; information

Mercury is considered the first of the inner planets because it is the planet closest to the Sun. Because of this solar proximity, the size of its ecliptic is the smallest, making it the fastest-moving planet. Mercury is known as "quicksilver," Hermes, and the fleet-footed messenger of the gods, so it makes perfect sense that it moves so quickly, changing signs roughly every 13–14 days. The exception to this rule would be Mercury's quarterly retrograde periods when it appears to move backward and takes around three and a half weeks to make its transit.

Because Mercury moves so closely to the Sun, you will notice your Mercury sign may be the same as your Sun sign or fall one to two signs away.

Mercury reflects how we communicate and process information, as well as how we form our ideas and our overall mental outlook. Look to your Mercury sign and the house it resides in to show you how you take in and express information and ideas, the type of student you are or were, and what you are meant to share with others in this lifetime.

MERCURY IN ARIES

KEY WORDS: hasty; pioneering

Mercury in Aries is a true initiator of ideas. This Mercury placement is ruled by fiery Mars, giving you a fast-paced intellect that makes you the first to express your thoughts and opinions and leap into action to execute them. You express yourself openly and directly, always saying exactly what's on your mind. While you may come off as impulsive or brash, people appreciate that they always know where they stand with you.

MERCURY IN TAURUS

KEY WORDS: practical; refined

Mercury in Taurus has a calm, steady mind. This Mercury placement is ruled by beautiful Venus, giving you the patience to make decisions without feeling rushed, stressed, or anxious, which other Mercury signs may experience. You express yourself in a confident, practical, yet refined manner, while your connection to the earth element helps ground your ideas so you can easily turn them into reality.

MERCURY IN GEMINI

KEY WORDS: chatty; curious

Mercury in Gemini finds itself in its home sign, as Gemini is ruled by Mercury. This placement gives you a sharp intellect, quick wit, and the ability to assimilate information at lightning speed. You may experience anxious thoughts, since your mind is constantly churning, so it may be helpful for you to write, journal, or talk through your ideas with others. You express yourself enthusiastically and experience the world with unending curiosity. You want to know everything about everything and everyone.

MERCURY IN CANCER

KEY WORDS: intuitive; sentimental

Mercury in Cancer gives emotional depth to your ideas and deep sentiment to the words you speak. This Mercury placement is ruled by the Moon and gives you incredibly intuitive mental powers, allowing you to feel information as you process the world around you. You express yourself in a warm, nurturing fashion. Unafraid to tackle heavy topics of conversation, you prefer deep talks that connect you to others rather than superficial interactions.

MERCURY IN LEO

KEY WORDS: bold; visionary

Mercury in Leo loves big, exciting ideas! Ruled by the Sun, this Mercury placement can dream bigger than most, though seeing the bigger picture can cause you to skip over or miss out on important details. There is a boldness to your speech as you express your visionary ideas that enables you to get almost anyone else on board with your intentions. Challenge yourself to take the time to listen to other people's ideas and opinions, especially when they differ from your own.

MERCURY IN VIRGO

KEY WORDS: focused; detail-oriented

Mercury in Virgo gifts you with incredible focus and attention to detail. Ruled by Mercury, this placement is in its home sign, offering you the most potent energy of Mercury in all forms of communication. Your mind is one of your greatest assets, as you can comprehend and assimilate information at an impressive rapid pace. You also benefit from the earthiness of Virgo, which lends practicality and groundedness to your sharp mind.

MERCURY IN LIBRA

KEY WORDS: charming; diplomatic

Mercury in well-mannered, charming Libra loves to schmooze and connect with others. This placement is ruled by beautiful Venus, who showers you with eloquence and appealing mannerisms that make you quite popular in your social circles. You are able to get along with almost anyone and are an expert at diffusing difficult situations because you help others see both sides of the conversation. You also may possess innate talents for writing, speech, singing, or poetry.

MERCURY IN SCORPIO

KEY WORDS: secretive; investigator

Mercury in mysterious Scorpio is the ultimate secret keeper. Ruled classically by Mars and modernly by Pluto, this placement gives you a calculating mind that penetrates deep. Your intuition, along with your desire to uncover hidden truths, makes you a talented researcher of any subject you choose, especially anything taboo or occult related. You value honesty and seek intimacy and connection in your communications, and you never shy away from deep conversation.

MERCURY IN SAGITTARIUS

KEY WORDS: broad-minded; curious

Mercury in adventurous Sagittarius is a curious thrill-seeker in search of new horizons. This Mercury placement is ruled by expansive Jupiter, giving you a universal love of knowledge and learning. You may find yourself interested in spirituality and world cultures, especially those that differ from how you grew up. The meaning of life excites you, and the pursuit of finding your truth is a lifelong quest for you. You benefit from staying open to ideas that differ from your personal philosophies.

MERCURY IN CAPRICORN

KEY WORDS: practical; reliable

Mercury in stoic Capricorn gives you the reliability to follow through with what you say you will do, allowing others to have the utmost trust in you. This placement is ruled by task-oriented Saturn, bringing the energy of hard work and dependability to your mental process and communications with others. Taking calculated risks generally pays off for you, due to the careful consideration you pay before taking action. You may not be overly sentimental in your speech, but your honest and direct approach is appreciated.

MERCURY IN AQUARIUS

KEY WORDS: observant; contrarian

Mercury in rebellious Aquarius prefers progressive discourse when it comes to communication. This placement is ruled classically by Saturn and modernly by Uranus, which gives you a unique blend of social responsibility and sometimes shocking unpredictability. You're intelligent and mentally sharp, with a tendency toward taking a logical approach to your progressive thinking that comes off as contrarian to others, making it impossible to pin you down or put you into any one box.

MERCURY IN PISCES

KEY WORDS: intuitive; imaginative

Mercury in ethereal Pisces defies logic, tending toward nonverbal communication and psychic impressions rather than objective truths. While Mercury rules our communication, ideas, and thinking, this placement—classically ruled by Jupiter and modernly by Neptune—is connected to the subconscious realm, allowing you to perceive thoughts through your feelings. Having your Mercury in Pisces endows you with deep creativity, allowing you to express yourself through art, poetry, and music as you channel higher realms.

Working with My Birth Chart: My Mercury

1. What is your Mercury sign?

   ....

2. Which house does your Mercury fall in and which zodiac sign is the natural ruler of that house?

   ....

3. Compare the key words of your Mercury sign and the natural house ruler (page 26). What insights does that provide you?

   ....

   ....

   ....

   ....

   ....

REFLECTION

How do you feel your Mercury placement impacts the way you communicate? How can you take the wisdom from your Mercury placement and apply it to the ways you share and receive information?

....

....

....

....

VENUS ♀

KEY WORDS: love; beauty; value

Venus is the second of the inner planets, since it is the second planet from the Sun. Because of its solar proximity, the size of its ecliptic orbit is slightly larger than Mercury's, making it the second-fastest-moving planet, taking roughly two to three weeks to transit each sign. Venus experiences its own retrograde every 18 months, in which Venus will stay in a particular sign for up to five months, asking us to reevaluate our finances and relationships.

Venus is the archetypal planet of love, beauty, art, and money, which rules over our relationships and how we relate to one another as well as what we love and value. Your Venus sign and the house it resides in will tell you all about what attracts you to others, as well as what other people find naturally attractive about you. This is helpful for understanding your core needs when it comes to loving relationships.

Your Venus sign will also offer insight into how you earn your money, your artistic gifts, and where abundance shines in your chart, just waiting for you to discover it!

VENUS IN ARIES

KEY WORDS: the lover and the fighter

Venus in fiery Aries burns hot and heavy when it comes to romance and relationships. This placement is ruled by feisty Mars, giving you the energy to pursue your pleasures with fervor. You never hesitate to initiate when going after love or money, making you incredibly persistent when you have your eye on a prize. The thrill of the chase is often what excites you, and you may change course once you've got what you've been pursuing. Abundance is found through taking initiative and going after what you want.

VENUS IN TAURUS

KEY WORDS: slow-and-sensual steady

Venus in slow, romantic Taurus values luxury as much as stability when it comes to romance and relationships. Venus is in its home sign and comfortable to be in Taurus, delighting in all the earthly pleasures. You are refined and romantic by nature, and settling isn't your style. You have infinite patience when it comes to both love and money. You are worth the wait, and you know what is worth waiting for. When you do commit, it's for the long haul. Abundance is found through a methodical approach to opulence.

VENUS IN GEMINI

KEY WORDS: flirtatious and fun

Venus in fun-loving, flirtatious Gemini is witty and curious by nature. This placement is ruled by intelligent Mercury, making intellectual stimulation a must when it comes to romance and relationships. You are an exceptional conversationalist and require great communication in your partnerships in order to keep them going, since you tend to lose interest once your curiosity is satisfied, moving on to new endeavors. Abundance is found through speaking things into existence; setting intentions is powerful for you.

VENUS IN CANCER

KEY WORDS: sensitive and sentimental

Venus in emotional Cancer is nurturing and caring when it comes to romance and relationships. This placement is ruled by the Moon, making emotional intelligence your greatest strength when it comes to love and money and also what you crave in return. You are tender, affectionate, and cherish sentimental moments. Your sensitivity does cause you to take things personally sometimes, leading to hurt feelings. Sharing how you feel helps you process your emotions. Abundance is found through embracing the vast range of your emotions and trusting your instincts.

VENUS IN LEO

KEY WORDS: opulent and affectionate

Venus in regal Leo loves grand gestures and opulent displays of adoration when it comes to romance and relationships. This placement is ruled by the Sun, and like the brightest luminary in the galaxy, your expressions of love and your relationship to money are big and bold, including your spending habits! Bigger is always better for Venus in Leo, sometimes including the drama you cook up around your relationships and finances. Despite the occasional spectacle, you love the pure, true concept of love, and it shows. Abundance is found through expressing your joy and enthusiasm, especially when uplifting those around you.

VENUS IN VIRGO

KEY WORDS: obliging perfectionist

Venus in analytical Virgo has a tendency to critique their partners as much as themselves when it comes to romance and relationships. This placement is ruled by intellectual Mercury, keeping your brain buzzing with ways to improve your existence when it comes to love and money, since being indispensable is a turn-on for you. Your health is important to you, and you love taking care of everything from your body to your plants, activities that help ground your thoughts and connect you with the present moment. Abundance is found through allowing yourself to receive as much as you give.

VENUS IN LIBRA

KEY WORDS: aesthetically pleasing and flirtatious

Venus is at home in charming Libra, where achieving harmony and balance are vital in romance and relationships. Ruled by Venus, this Libra placement loves to be surrounded by beauty. From your partners and the way they dress to your home decor and surroundings, aesthetics are everything. Despite your flirty nature, you enjoy being part of a duo, especially when the partnership thrives on luxury and cooperation. Your only shortcoming may be the occasional bout of indecision, as you are usually trying to please everyone. Abundance is found through your eye for beauty and the ability to be charming in any situation.

VENUS IN SCORPIO

KEY WORDS: passionate and intense

Venus in obsessive Scorpio is a sexy tour through the mysterious depths of the ocean when it comes to romance and relationships. This placement is ruled classically by Mars and modernly by Pluto, giving you an intensity that requires loyalty and passion when it comes to love and money. Casual encounters are not your style. You are intuitive and sensitive, working hard to protect your heart, which means you may fall fast, then test your lovers to make sure they are worthy of your powerful love. Abundance is found through your natural magnetism and willingness to surrender and transform.

VENUS IN SAGITTARIUS

KEY WORDS: enthusiastic and adventurous

Venus in freedom-loving Sagittarius doesn't like to be tied down. This placement is ruled by expansive Jupiter, giving you insatiable wanderlust when it comes to romance and relationships. This doesn't mean you aren't capable of commitment; it just means you crave excitement and adventure in matters of love and money. Partnerships that support growth and learning will keep your interest, as you express your need to explore new horizons. Abundance is found through your enthusiastic pursuit of adventure and navigating your personal path of truth.

VENUS IN CAPRICORN

KEY WORDS: consistent and committed

Venus in hardworking Capricorn is committed to building solid foundations when it comes to romance and relationships. This placement is ruled by restrictive Saturn, which gives you a slow, cautious approach to love and money. You want a partner who is serious about their goals and ambitions and who will support yours in return. Casual encounters aren't your style; you require stability and won't waste your time on flaky or indecisive connections. Abundance is found through determination and perseverance as you reach your long-term goals.

VENUS IN AQUARIUS

KEY WORDS: independent and quirky

Venus in Aquarius is a true individual who breaks the mold in romance and relationships. This placement is classically ruled by Saturn and modernly by Uranus, making you unpredictable and independent in matters of love and money. You value mental stimulation as well as individuality in others and appreciate those who understand your futuristic outlook and unique qualities. You may place greater emphasis on friendship over romantic relationships and require freedom from your partners from time to time. Abundance is found in your individuality and sharing your innovative ideas.

VENUS IN PISCES

KEY WORDS: romantic and generous

Venus in self-sacrificing Pisces loves the concept of love itself. This placement is ruled classically by Jupiter and modernly by Neptune, giving you all of the expansive nebulous gifts of dreamy romance and idealized relationships. You are able to see the beauty in everything and everyone, turning your vision into artistic expression when it comes to love and money. Your intuition, compassion, and overall ethereal quality draw others to you easily, yet may leave you vulnerable to being hurt when they aren't as open and honest as you are. Abundance is found through your psychic senses and dreams.

Working with My Birth Chart: My Venus

1. What is your Venus sign?

    ....

2. Which house does your Venus fall in and which zodiac sign is the natural ruler of that house?

    ....

3. Compare the key words of your Venus sign and the natural house ruler (page 26). What insights does that provide you?

    ....

    ....

    ....

    ....

    ....

REFLECTION

How do you feel your Venus placement impacts how you approach love and relationships? How can you distinguish between your personal values and what you value in others based on your Venus sign?

....

....

....

....

MARS ♂

KEY WORDS: action; drive; desire

Mars is the third and final of the inner planets, as it is close enough to the Sun that its ecliptic orbit is larger than Mercury and Venus, making it the third-fastest-moving planet, taking roughly two months to transit each sign. Mars experiences its own retrograde every two years. During this time, Mars will stay in a particular sign for up to seven months, asking us collectively and personally to reevaluate how we take action and express anger, as well as where we need course correction.

Mars is the archetypal planet of war, aggression, action, and pure animal passion, which rules over our anger, our sex drive, how we argue, and how we take action in the world. Your Mars sign and the house it resides in will tell you about your anger and how you express it, as well as how you take action toward your goals and stick up for yourself. While your Venus sign represents what you're attracted to and what you value, your Mars sign will reveal how you are in bed and what you want from your romantic partners to have the fulfilling sex life you deserve.

MARS IN ARIES

KEY WORDS: ardent; assertive

Mars is at home in fiery Aries, its ruling planet, giving you incredible action-oriented energy to charge ahead toward any goal. You are confident and driven to succeed at everything you tackle, from the boardroom to the bedroom. Your passion for taking the lead boosts your confidence and fuels your inner fire to pursue anything you set your mind to achieve. When it comes to your sexual preferences, you are an ardent lover who goes after what they want. You value direct communication and enjoy the process of pursuing what you want more than committing once you get it.

MARS IN TAURUS

KEY WORDS: patient; determined

Mars in steadfast Taurus helps the planet of impulse and action slow down and put energy into what it truly values. This placement is ruled by gentle Venus, bestowing a softness to the usually aggressive nature of Mars. While you aren't easily provoked, once you hit your threshold, your potent temper is revealed. When it comes to your sexual needs and desires, you are an earthy, sensual lover who takes their time in the bedroom. You value patience and stamina and prefer not to be rushed when taking action, which your lovers adore about you.

MARS IN GEMINI

KEY WORDS: gossip; multitasking

Mars in mentally agile Gemini gives you a witty and curious nature that expresses itself through the mind, since this placement is ruled by Mercury. With the planet of action in the sign of communication, you have a talent for multitasking, and when provoked, you use your words as ammunition better than any other sign. Watch out for gossiping when you get bored; try to redirect your cognitive skills to something more productive. When it comes to your sexual needs and desires, you must be turned on mentally first. Intelligent conversation and lots of kissing are both musts.

MARS IN CANCER

KEY WORDS: protective; emotional

Mars in sensitive Cancer is fiercely loyal and protective of their loved ones. This placement is ruled by the Moon, and your emotions will dictate your actions, fluctuating from angry and aggressive to sensitive and passive, all in a matter of minutes. You are meant to feel a wide range of emotions in response to your surroundings. Whenever possible, try to wait until you find yourself back at neutral before taking action. When it comes to your sexual needs and desires, taking on the role of nurturer turns you on since you require a deep emotional connection with your partners.

MARS IN LEO

KEY WORDS: confident; charismatic

Mars in showy Leo loves to express itself, and the world is its audience. With the Sun ruling this placement, you tend to do everything with a flair for the dramatic. Your love of drama extends to your fiery temper, though your natural enthusiasm and warmth mitigate the occasional angry outburst. When it comes to your sexual needs and desires, you love to make fantasies a reality, creating romantic scenarios and acting them out playfully and passionately. You may also enjoy sex in front of the mirror or the thrill of being filmed.

MARS IN VIRGO

KEY WORDS: organized; devoted

Mars in analytical Virgo has an eye for details and a mind for organization. This placement is ruled by Mercury, giving you mental productivity and the earthly grounding to get things done efficiently. You may be more critical than aggressive when it comes to your temperament, but you offer your opinions with everyone's best interest in mind. When it comes to your sexual needs and desires, you understand that sex is a form of stress relief and a key component to a healthy lifestyle. You're eager to please your lovers and aren't as picky in the bedroom as other Virgo placements.

MARS IN LIBRA

KEY WORDS: harmony; balance

Mars in equality-seeking Libra is the peacemaker of Mars placements, as this placement is ruled by gentle Venus. You have a natural inclination toward peaceful resolution rather than arguments and will take a passive approach to getting things done. No one should mistake your kindness for weakness, since you are incredibly charming and persuasive. When it comes to your sexual needs and desires, you prefer the right aesthetic atmosphere for making love and require fairness and equal giving and receiving in the bedroom.

MARS IN SCORPIO

KEY WORDS: instinctive; magnetic

Mars in powerful, private Scorpio is a driven investigator, since this placement is ruled classically by Mars and modernly by Pluto. You feel a deep need for intensity and take emotionally driven action toward anything you truly desire. You have natural insight into the motivations of others, giving you a magnetic presence that is both intense and alluring. When it comes to your sexual needs and desires, you crave intimacy and passion and are willing to push yourself and your lovers to shatter taboos in the pursuit of pleasure.

MARS IN SAGITTARIUS

KEY WORDS: adventurous; energetic

Mars in intrepid Sagittarius takes wanderlust to new levels. This placement is ruled by expansive Jupiter, making you a philosophical seeker in constant search for what lies beyond the literal and metaphorical horizon. You are attached to your ideals and will argue your point with fervor. When it comes to your sexual needs and desires, you approach intimacy with the same energetic enthusiasm you bring to the rest of your life, making you a ton of fun in bed. While you're here for a good time, it's not usually a long time since freedom is your love language.

MARS IN CAPRICORN

KEY WORDS: determined; committed

Mars in ambitious Capricorn is driven to succeed at all costs. This placement is ruled by restrictive Saturn, making you an expert of delayed gratification. You strive to be the best at everything you do and hold yourself to incredibly high standards. When it comes to your sexual needs and desires, you approach intimacy with the same determination and stamina as the rest of your life. You work hard to please your partner and make a generous and devoted lover.

MARS IN AQUARIUS

KEY WORDS: eccentric; idealistic

Mars in quirky Aquarius gives an unusual approach to taking action. This placement is classically ruled by Saturn and modernly by Uranus, making you committed to your progressive ideas. Your approach may be unorthodox, but your intellect and communication skills help you get your point across. When it comes to your sexual needs and desires, you are open-minded and adventurous and prefer spontaneity and experimentation in the bedroom. You'll try anything once; just don't repeat it more than twice.

MARS IN PISCES

KEY WORDS: compassionate; emotional

Mars in empathetic Pisces champions the downtrodden. This placement is ruled classically by Jupiter and modernly by Neptune, giving you a mild temperament that borders on passive, unless you feel emotionally connected to a situation that drives you to take action. When it comes to your sexual needs and desires, you are a generous lover who works hard to please your partner. Your incredible intuition leads you to know instinctively what turns them on, making the art of giving its own reward for you.

Working with My Birth Chart: My Mars

1. What is your Mars sign?

   ....

2. Which house does your Mars fall in and which zodiac sign is the natural ruler of that house?

   ....

3. Compare the key words of your Mars sign and the natural house ruler (page 26). What insights does that provide you?

   ....

   ....

   ....

   ....

   ....

REFLECTION

How do you feel your Mars placement impacts how you take action and how you handle conflict? How can you be better equipped to manage strong emotions when facing conflict based on your Mars placement?

....

....

....

....

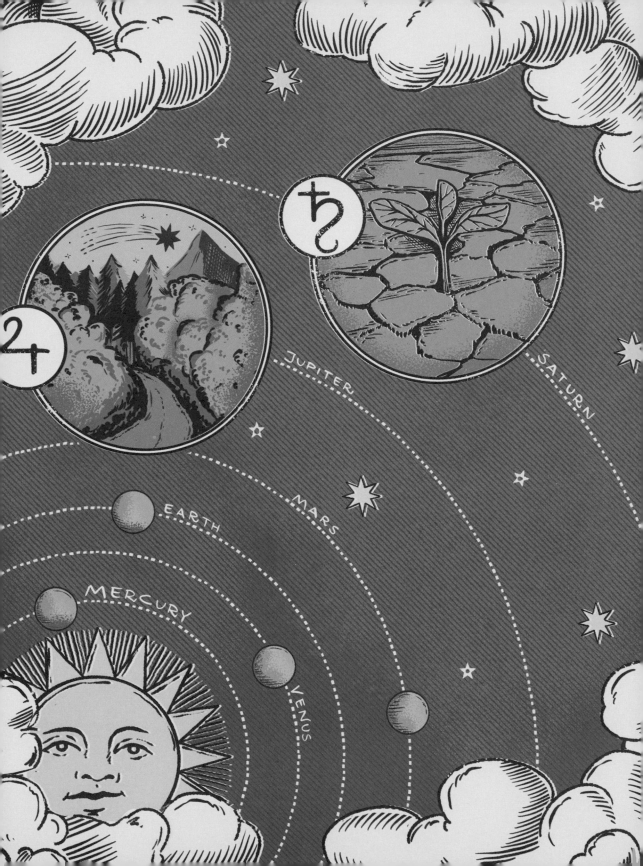

SEVEN

Harnessing the Social Planets

. . . .

NOW WE'RE MOVING farther out into our galaxy, and in tandem we're starting to explore concepts in your chart that are a little bit removed from your core identity. Beyond the inner planets lie the two social planets, Jupiter and Saturn. Their orbits along the ecliptic take longer than Mercury, Venus, and Mars due to their distance from the Sun, altering the effect they have on us personally and collectively. Due to their longer-range effects on a large group of people at once, they are considered social rather than inner or personal planets.

Jupiter and Saturn play pivotal roles in your personal development, how you progress through life, and the role you are here to play within society. Understanding the sign and house in which your social planets fall will help you understand where you experience ease and good luck, as well as where you experience challenges. This knowledge enables you to harness the power within you to overcome and integrate life lessons on the physical and spiritual planes. Learning about your social planetary placements will help you grow and expand into the most integrated version of yourself in this lifetime.

JUPITER ♃

KEY WORDS: good fortune; luck; expansion

Jupiter, the first of the social planets and largest planet in our solar system, takes approximately one year to transit through each sign and retrogrades for four to five months. During this time, we are asked to reevaluate our spirituality, personal growth, how we expand, and where we want to go next.

Your Jupiter sign and the house it falls within can tell you about your personal path to growth as it relates to philosophy and spirituality, how you expand your worldview, your views on long-distance and foreign travel, and your approach to higher education. Look to Jupiter to show you how you experience good fortune and lucky breaks, since Jupiter expands whatever it touches. This area of your chart will show you where you can harness that expansive energy for your benefit.

JUPITER IN ARIES

KEY WORDS: confident; crusader

Jupiter in action-oriented Aries is the ultimate go-getter. With Mars ruling this placement, you are confident and driven to succeed. Expansive Jupiter bestows you with boundless energy and self-motivation to experience life as an adventure. Learning new skills and information fuels your love of self-directed discovery. Lucky breaks and good fortune favor all you do when you center yourself and prioritize your own growth, motivating others with your pioneering spirit.

JUPITER IN TAURUS

KEY WORDS: grounded pleasure-seeker

Jupiter in Taurus may be stable and practical, but it is anything but boring. Ruled by romantic Venus, this placement puts the pursuit of pleasure at the forefront of your adventurous quests. Grounded earth energy brings you the patience needed to make your dreams into reality, while expansive Jupiter brings you good fortune and lucky breaks when it comes to the material side of life. From finances to fine dining, the world is your oyster.

JUPITER IN GEMINI

KEY WORDS: curious conversationalist

Jupiter in chatty Gemini is a curious seeker of knowledge and information. Ruled by inquisitive Mercury, this placement gives you a broad intellect coupled with a tenacious appetite for media and communication of all kinds. Expansive, optimistic Jupiter brings you good fortune and lucky opportunities in the areas of reading, public speaking, and writing, inviting you to share your gift of gab with the collective.

JUPITER IN CANCER

KEY WORDS: emotionally intelligent nurturer

Jupiter in emotional Cancer is an empathetic caregiver. Ruled by the intuitive Moon, this placement gives you clear insight into the emotional needs of others and the skills to provide ideal support in any situation. Helping others is its own reward, and expansive Jupiter brings you waves of good fortune and lucky opportunities when you are sharing your big, beautiful heart with the collective.

JUPITER IN LEO

KEY WORDS: enthusiastic creator

Jupiter in dramatic Leo is joyfully expressive. This placement is ruled by the Sun, giving you an air of regality that is amplified by Jupiter's larger-than-life energy. Your charismatic persona is best received when you remember to shine your light on everyone rather than centering it on yourself. Expansive opportunities and lucky breaks come through your creative pursuits and sharing your genuine enthusiasm for life with the collective.

JUPITER IN VIRGO

KEY WORDS: diligent and patient worker

Jupiter in analytical Virgo seeks to achieve success through hard work and perseverance. This placement is ruled by intelligent Mercury, giving you the mental agility and practicality to make your dreams a reality. Expansive Jupiter will bring you lucky opportunities and good fortune; however, it requires an optimistic outlook alongside concentrated effort on your part to bring them into fruition.

JUPITER IN LIBRA

KEY WORDS: diplomatic partner

Jupiter in balanced Libra seeks harmony through partnership in both love and business. This placement is ruled by lovely Venus, gifting you with charm and the ability to see the beauty in any situation. Expansive Jupiter helps you easily find luck in love and romance as well as in your business ventures. Smooth communication comes naturally to you, making you popular and well-liked among your peers.

JUPITER IN SCORPIO

KEY WORDS: magnetic and secretive dreamer

Jupiter in private, introspective Scorpio is a silent powerhouse. This placement is classically ruled by Mars and modernly by Pluto, giving you the drive to seek out your dreams and put everything you've got into achieving them through your natural ability to attract resources. Expansive Jupiter brings lucky opportunities and good fortune when you combine your strong intuition with sheer willpower to make magic happen.

JUPITER IN SAGITTARIUS

KEY WORDS: lucky adventurer

Jupiter in optimistic Sagittarius is one of the luckiest places to be, as Jupiter is in its home sign, giving you boundless enthusiasm that naturally attracts good fortune, lucky breaks, and exciting opportunities. You have an adventurous spirit with a love of travel, learning, and expanding your worldview. Abundant Jupiter brings prosperous opportunities through sharing your knowledge with others, so always let yourself remain open-minded and enthusiastic.

JUPITER IN CAPRICORN

KEY WORDS: methodical strategist

Jupiter in somber Capricorn is driven and ambitious. This placement is ruled by restrictive Saturn, giving you the focus and determination to bring your goals and dreams to fruition through careful planning and strategy. Expansive Jupiter brings lucky opportunities and good fortune when you are focused and realistic about your plans and remembering to be generous with others while achieving your own success.

JUPITER IN AQUARIUS

KEY WORDS: social justice innovator

Jupiter in freedom-loving Aquarius wants innovative reform for the collective rather than purely personal gain. This placement is ruled classically by Saturn and modernly by Uranus, giving you a sense of social responsibility and futuristic outlook on where the collective should be heading. Expansive Jupiter brings good fortune and lucky opportunities when you are interacting with like-minded individuals, coming together for the greater good.

JUPITER IN PISCES

KEY WORDS: compassionate; intuitive

Jupiter in empathetic Pisces amplifies the connection to universal love. This placement is classically ruled by Jupiter itself and modernly by Neptune, giving you remarkable intuition accompanied by a strong spiritual sense that transcends the earthly realm. Expansive Jupiter brings wonderful opportunities and good luck when you pay attention to your intuition, heed your dreams, and tap into your natural creativity.

Working with My Birth Chart: My Jupiter

1. What is your Jupiter sign?

   ....

2. Which house does your Jupiter fall in and which zodiac sign is the natural ruler of that house?

   ....

3. Compare the key words of your Jupiter sign and the natural house ruler (page 26). What insights does that provide you?

   ....

   ....

   ....

   ....

   ....

REFLECTION

How do you feel your Jupiter placement has brought unforeseen luck and abundance to you? What has your Jupiter sign taught you about your own sense of spirituality?

....

....

....

....

SATURN ♄

KEY WORDS: discipline; restriction; responsibility

Saturn, the other social planet, takes up to two and a half years to transit each sign and has a retrograde period of four to five months. During a Saturn retrograde, we are asked to reevaluate the work we put into our goals and how we've been taking responsibility for our role in our lives and society.

Your Saturn sign may seem like a bummer, showing you where you experience restriction, delays, and separation; however, this is for karmic purposes specific to you in this lifetime. Your Saturn sign and the house it resides within will show you what your most important work is, challenges and obstacles to overcome, and the path to maturing and becoming more responsible as you progress through life. Saturn teaches you that your greatest hindrances are by showing you your most valuable assets. It's important to remember that Saturn always rewards hard work and dedication.

SATURN IN ARIES

KEY WORDS: self-disciplined; confrontational

Saturn in self-focused Aries asks you to develop self-discipline through restriction of your personal freedom or physical body. This placement is ruled by fiery Mars, meaning you may experience challenges with leadership, having a temper, or being generally overbearing. Cultivating responsibility for your behavior is a lifelong process that will transform how you manage your relationships with others. This holds true both from a leadership perspective and in terms of becoming the captain of your own life.

SATURN IN TAURUS

KEY WORDS: security-driven; loyal

Saturn in dependable Taurus craves stability and certainty when it comes to physical resources. This placement is ruled by Venus, placing an emphasis on the material side of life. Sometimes it may feel like you never have enough, despite being financially stable. Cultivating an understanding of life's value beyond your bank account is part of your purpose. Focus on creating strong self-worth through your reliability and dedication to long-term goals, trusting that you are capable of generating everything you need.

SATURN IN GEMINI

KEY WORDS: fact-driven; intellectual

Saturn in intellectual Gemini asks you to develop structure and organization to your thoughts, which tend to be all over the place. Ruled by lightning-fast Mercury, you have a sharp mind that is constantly racing. Cultivating healthy habits around focusing your mind and your relationship to media is a lifelong practice that will help you communicate your ideas and declutter your mental space. Doing this improves your self-esteem, giving you confidence in yourself rather than overemphasizing facts.

SATURN IN CANCER

KEY WORDS: emotional; intuitive

Saturn in sensitive Cancer challenges you to balance your emotions with practicality. This placement is ruled by the Moon, causing you to be driven by instincts and feelings rather than serious reasoning. You feel a sense of responsibility to your friends and family or to the home and can have a tendency to shut down your feelings in favor of nurturing others. Cultivating the healthy expression of your emotions (while not allowing them to overtake you) is extremely rewarding, since you nourish your close relationships.

SATURN IN LEO

KEY WORDS: proud; self-critical

Saturn in energetic Leo asks you to learn how to balance work and play. Ruled by the vibrant Sun, this placement restricts the expression of your larger-than-life personality. You may feel frustrated and overlooked but unable to convey your brilliance to others out of fear of not being well received. These lessons are teaching you to cultivate vulnerability and release rigidity as you confidently find your path to joy and creative self-expression. You are meant to be seen and heard.

SATURN IN VIRGO

KEY WORDS: pragmatic; efficient

Saturn in practical Virgo asks you to develop your personal power while acting in service to others in a way that feels authentic and joyful (rather than taken advantage of). This placement is ruled by analytical Mercury, giving you a sharp mental capacity for problem-solving that you readily share with others. Acknowledging and prioritizing your own issues will help you cultivate confidence and kick-start the process of self-healing, making you available and better equipped to help others.

SATURN IN LIBRA

KEY WORDS: agreeable; rational

Saturn in harmony-loving Libra asks you to develop balance in your relationships. Ruled by beautiful Venus, this placement makes you nonconfrontational, seeking peaceful resolutions at the cost of your own needs and boundaries. These lessons are teaching you the importance of self-assertion to maintain healthy relationships while cultivating self-respect. Becoming responsible for making decisions and speaking up for yourself are the path to more peaceful, loving connections.

SATURN IN SCORPIO

KEY WORDS: willful; resourceful

Saturn in secretive Scorpio asks you to confront and eliminate the distractions that cloud your vision of your goals. This intense placement is classically ruled by Mars and modernly by Pluto, giving you ruthless ambition and focus on achieving your desires. Success and maturity are achieved through cultivating a healthy sense of your own limitations and altruistic motives in pursuing power and authority. You are a force to be reckoned with, so use your powers for good and good will come to you.

SATURN IN SAGITTARIUS

KEY WORDS: independent; philosophical

Saturn in adventurous Sagittarius challenges you to explore life within responsible boundaries. This placement is ruled by expansive Jupiter, creating a push-pull effect that restricts your personal freedom for the purpose of helping you mature. Cultivating a strong sense of ethics and knowledge of the topics that light you up leads you to climb great heights. This wisdom helps you achieve your goals and access the freedom that once felt out of your grasp. Sharing your experiences and expertise with others is an important contribution to your relationships.

SATURN IN CAPRICORN

KEY WORDS: mature; ambitious

Saturn is at home in responsible Capricorn, asking you to achieve your ambitions through dedication and hard work. Ruled by restrictive Saturn, this placement understands that the bigger the challenge, the greater the reward. You may experience setbacks and delays on your quest to achieve your goals, but these lessons are teaching you how to find balance between attainment and rest. Cultivating self-care and allowing yourself to relax and enjoy life will lead to great personal fulfillment.

SATURN IN AQUARIUS

KEY WORDS: free-thinking; humanitarian

Saturn in open-minded Aquarius asks you to contribute meaningfully to society by learning how to balance leadership and group dynamics with loving and caring for yourself. This placement is classically ruled by Saturn and modernly by Uranus, giving you incredible focus and ambition to share your innovative ideas with others. You have natural leadership skills and the ability to take on many tasks at once. Cultivating a sense of self-care and boundaries will improve your relationships and alleviate burnout.

SATURN IN PISCES

KEY WORDS: dreamer; doer

Saturn in dreamy Pisces asks you to make your dreams a reality through cultivating responsibility and groundedness on the physical plane. This placement is classically ruled by expansive Jupiter and modernly by nebulous Neptune, giving you tremendous access to creativity and a rich fantasy world. These traits lead you to create tangible results with Saturn's tough love. Your spirituality is the grounding practice that will help you navigate the darker side of the human experience.

Working with Your Birth Chart: My Saturn

1. What is your Saturn sign?

    ....

2. Which house does your Saturn fall in and which zodiac sign is the natural ruler of that house?

    ....

3. Compare the key words of your Saturn sign and the natural house ruler (page 26). What insights does that provide you?

    ....

    ....

    ....

    ....

    ....

REFLECTION

What restrictions, boundaries, or lessons has your Saturn placement brought you? How have they benefited you in terms of cultivating greater responsibility and growth?

....

....

....

....

NOTES

NEPTUNE

PLUTO

URANUS

EIGHT

Analyzing the Outer Planets

· · · · · · · · · · · · · · · · · · · ·

EVEN DISTANT COMMONALITIES affect us. People who grew up in the same state won't have as much in common as people who grew up in the same household, but they'll still have some important overlapping experiences and opinions! When we're exploring Sun and Moon signs, or even the inner planets, it's all about your own unique traits and needs.

As we travel even farther out into our galaxy to encounter the outer planets—Uranus, Neptune, and Pluto—we're starting to delve into commonalities at that more distant (but still significant) "grew up in the same state" level. These three planets are considered outer or "generational" planets due to their distance from the Sun. The movement along the ecliptic path for these planets is so slow that they affect us collectively rather than personally. While each of these planets will have a specific role to play in the unfolding of your birth, you will notice that they play a similar role in the lives of those born around the same time as you.

It is also important to note that while the inner planets (Mercury, Venus, and Mars) only take a matter of weeks to transit through each sign, and the social planets (Jupiter and Saturn) take up to two years, the outer planets take more than two years to make their way through each sign. This leisurely pace brings about gradual, long-term changes in your life that cannot be rushed. Understanding your Uranus, Neptune, and Pluto signs will help you understand and integrate the more esoteric roles you are here to embody during this lifetime and within our shared society.

URANUS ♅

KEY WORDS: freedom; change; uniqueness

Uranus, the first of the outer planets, is known in astrology as the "great awakener" whose energy liberates us from outmoded cycles we get stuck in throughout our lives. Mythologically connected to the god of the sky, Uranus represents our higher mind and expresses itself as the changes thrust upon us when we deviate from our path of individuality. This can manifest as a breakup, job loss, fluctuations in finances, or other sudden changes in circumstances. On a more positive note, Uranus also leads the evolution of society in terms of technological innovations.

Understanding your Uranus sign and the house in which it resides will empower you to turn seemingly unfortunate events into opportunities to grow and express your uniqueness. Uranus in your birth chart by sign and house will show you the area of life in which you're most likely to experience great change. While this change is sometimes shocking, it leads to a greater sense of freedom and liberation.

Uranus spends roughly seven years in each sign, and during that time it will have an effect on the collective as well as in your personal life. Look to Uranus to guide you to greater independence through expressing your individuality.

URANUS IN ARIES

DATES: 1927–1935; 2010–2019

Uranus in Aries, the sign of the self, brings great change in the way you assert and present yourself, most recently on social media and through personal technology. Think selfies, personal devices, and carefully curated self-branding. Ruled by Mars, this placement is about asserting yourself as a leader, content creator, or influencer. Break free of anything that constricts your sense of freedom so individual self-expression can lead you to greater integration and fulfillment.

URANUS IN TAURUS

DATES: 1935–1942; 2019–2026

Uranus in Taurus—the sign of values, your possessions, and creating material stability—brings great change in your sense of self-worth and what it means to feel secure in the physical world. Ruled by beautiful Venus, this placement impacts what you value and how you earn money. Fluctuations in personal finances can occur as you puzzle out what wealth represents for you, both spiritually and materially, by breaking free from tradition and societal expectation.

URANUS IN GEMINI

DATES: 1942–1949

Uranus in Gemini, the sign of communication and the mind, brings great changes in how you were raised to think and the development of your individual thought processes. This placement is ruled by intellectual Mercury and gives you a sharp mind with the ability to understand the paradoxes that exist within yourself and society, leading to a revolutionary outlook that should be shared with the collective. Breaking free of confining ideas and dogmatic principles will lead to a greater sense of personal freedom.

URANUS IN CANCER

DATES: 1948–1956

Uranus in Cancer, the sign of the home and family structure, brings great changes in how you approach building a home and the way you nurture your own family. This placement is ruled by the Moon and brings a fluctuation to the emotional intelligence needed for you to grow and create your own path, free from the confines of the past. Family values take on new meaning as you explore and experiment with alternative definitions of what home and family uniquely mean to you.

URANUS IN LEO

DATES: 1955–1962

Uranus in Leo, the sign of creativity and self-expression, brings great changes to how you share your creative gifts and talents with others. Ruled by the Sun, this placement asks you to break free from feeling self-conscious or afraid to pursue your dreams because of societal conditioning. Resist the temptation to follow the herd, and embrace your individuality no matter how eccentric or niche your talents may be. Following your passion to create is your ultimate path to fulfillment.

URANUS IN VIRGO

DATES: 1961–1969

Uranus in Virgo—the sign of healthy living and physical well-being through careful analysis of information—brings great change to the way you approach traditional health care and healing. Ruled by curious Mercury, this placement asks you to find a better way to care for your body by experimenting and thinking outside the box. Breaking free from old methods and routines will lead you on your unique path to discovering the true meaning of wellness and work-life balance for you.

URANUS IN LIBRA

DATES: 1968–1975

Uranus in Libra—the sign of love, harmony, and relationships—brings great changes to the way you approach partnerships and romance. Ruled by lovely Venus, this placement seeks equality and balance through finding new definitions for relationships that truly work for you individually. It can also mean revolutionizing what partnership means collectively. Breaking free from traditional marriage and heteronormative ideas will lead you to experience loving connections that suit you authentically.

URANUS IN SCORPIO

DATES: 1974–1981

Uranus in Scorpio—the sign of death, sexuality, and transformation—brings great changes to how you research and find new ways of approaching your sexuality and mortality. Ruled classically by Mars and modernly by Pluto, this placement asks you to find new ways of living by experiencing intensity and life-altering events. Scorpio energy needs to feel intensely and can handle the depths of the human experience. By embracing these moments, you find your path of acceptance and transformative fulfillment.

URANUS IN SAGITTARIUS

DATES: 1981–1988

Uranus in Sagittarius, the sign of personal philosophy and exploration, brings great changes in how you disrupt consensus-based thinking by living authentically and modeling this authenticity for society. Ruled by expansive Jupiter, this placement seeks an exciting lifestyle that breaks from tradition, including everything from religious freedom to alternative working environments. Achieving a blissful quality of life that is uniquely yours is the optimal path for you.

URANUS IN CAPRICORN

DATES: 1988–1996

Uranus in Capricorn, the sign of responsibility and hard work, brings changes to the very structure of society. Ruled by stoic Saturn, this placement seeks to reform an outdated dysfunctional society. Armed with patience and determination, you understand it takes time and much experimentation to find the optimal solutions. Breaking free from what isn't working may include demanding new options in health care, the education system, 40-plus-hour workweeks, or other aspects of life. You're here to optimize it all.

URANUS IN AQUARIUS

DATES: 1995–2003

Uranus in its home sign of Aquarius—the sign that rules technological advancements and humanitarian efforts—brings changes to how you evolve in ways that benefit you personally and also impact the collective. This placement has grown up with the internet, so technology is second nature to you. You can take the best of what technology has to offer and envision a better future by breaking free from focusing on the individual. Thinking globally and locally will lead to greater fulfillment.

URANUS IN PISCES

DATES: 2003–2011

Uranus in Pisces, the sign of mysticism and mental health, will influence how you approach the mind-body-spirit connection. Ruled classically by Jupiter and modernly by Neptune, this placement asks you to experiment with healing by combining spirituality with science to achieve new breakthroughs in personal development. Alternative forms of therapy and medicine will no longer be taboo as you find your unique path to healing yourself and society.

Working with My Birth Chart: My Uranus

1. What is your Uranus sign?

    ....

2. Which house does your Uranus fall in and which zodiac sign is the natural ruler of that house?

    ....

3. Compare the key words of your Uranus sign and the natural house ruler (page 26). What insights does that provide you?

    ....
    ....
    ....
    ....
    ....

REFLECTION

How has your Uranus placement brought change into your life? What unique qualities is your Uranus placement asking you to accept and engage with?

....
....
....
....

NEPTUNE ♆

KEY WORDS: dreams; illusions; idealism

Beyond Uranus lies Neptune, the second outer planet, which spends around 14 years in each sign, affecting you personally as well as collectively. Neptune is the lovingly compassionate planet associated with psychic abilities, intuition, and our dreams and fantasies, as well as self-destructive tendencies like escapism, deception, illusion, and delusions.

Mythologically associated with the deity for which it is named, Neptune, the god of the sea, the watery energy of Neptune is both slippery and foggy. It can cloud our judgment in ways that cause us to see the highest potential, even when it doesn't exist. There is also a tendency to see the lowest potential, real or imagined, in oneself and society that causes us to escape the depressive feelings accompanied by despair.

Understanding your Neptune sign and the house in which it resides will show you where you experience self-sabotage and escapism as well as confusion and illusion. On the positive side, your Neptune placement by house and sign will also show you where you experience intuitive abilities and creativity. Look to this placement to see how you can use these gifts to bring your visionary creations to life by tapping into the collective consciousness and your spirituality.

NEPTUNE IN ARIES

DATES: 1862–1875; 2025–2038

Neptune in Aries—the sign of war, aggression, and leadership—is driven to assert personal will, even if that means confrontation. Ruled by fiery Mars, this placement ruling self-sabotage, illusions, creativity, and intuition finds itself in a position to face conflict head-on. Neptune in Aries is not a historically peaceful time; however, transcendence is achieved by softening this energy and channeling it into new approaches toward mental health and personal healing.

NEPTUNE IN TAURUS

DATES: 1875–1889

Neptune in Taurus, the sign of wealth, stability, and sensual pleasure, can lead to overindulgence in the material side of life. Ruled by beautiful Venus, this placement seeks to meld the practical with the fanciful, leading to escapism through consumerism while trying to fill the emptiness that can only be satiated through spirituality. In Taurus there is an emphasis on transcendence by connecting with the Earth to ground the dreamy energy of Neptune.

NEPTUNE IN GEMINI

DATES: 1889–1902

Neptune in Gemini, the Mercury-ruled sign of communication and mental processing, finds itself able to take dreamy Neptunian fantasies and turn them into inventive realities. This placement is responsible for mental confusion and escapism through daydreaming as much as it is manifesting those creative visions to benefit society. Transcendence is achieved through connecting to the collective consciousness through blending creativity and critical thinking.

NEPTUNE IN CANCER

DATES: 1902–1915

Neptune in Cancer—the lunar-ruled sign of nurturing, the home, and family—meets with the equally intuitive qualities of Neptune, leading to new ways of caring for the family unit. Cancer energy can be manipulative and passive-aggressive, manifesting as illusion or escapism through indulging in unhealthy coping mechanisms to please others. Transcendence is achieved through endeavoring to see your family dynamics clearly rather than being overly empathic.

NEPTUNE IN LEO

DATES: 1915–1929

Neptune in Leo, the sign of enthusiastic and creative self-expression, finds itself idealistic to the point of delusion in this solar-ruled placement. Leo's prideful vision of taking center stage becomes overblown and unable to manifest itself in reality, leading to disappointment and disillusion. Transcendence is achieved by tapping into your gifts for drama and flair while maintaining spiritual balance and healthy ego perspective.

NEPTUNE IN VIRGO

DATES: 1928–1943

Neptune in Virgo, the Mercury-ruled sign of practicality and perfected health, finds itself challenged by the dreamy, abstract quality of Neptune. This placement is prone to confusion and escapism from daily tasks and responsibilities as well as sensitivities to substances or other unexplainable health concerns. Transcendence is achieved by balancing the need to be of service to others with a focus on your own life-management skills.

NEPTUNE IN LIBRA

DATES: 1942–1956

Neptune in Libra, the Venus-ruled sign of equality and peacekeeping within relationships, finds itself overgiving and self-sacrificing under Neptune's compassionate influence. This placement is romantic and idealistic about partnership and love. This means you may find yourself taken advantage of by significant others in ways you cannot see clearly. Transcendence is achieved by avoiding escapism and seeing relationships clearly rather than projecting a fantasy onto your partners.

NEPTUNE IN SCORPIO

DATES: 1956–1970

Neptune in Scorpio—the sign of secrecy, death, mystery, and sexual intimacy—finds itself swimming into the Neptunian depths of fantasy and dream analysis. Ruled by both Mars and Pluto, this placement longs to merge the spiritual with the physical and psychological through intense sensory experience with both sex and money. Transcendence is achieved through balancing your giving nature with receiving, while being aware of and setting clear boundaries.

NEPTUNE IN SAGITTARIUS

DATES: 1970–1984

Neptune in Sagittarius—the sign of seeking truth, adventure, and expansion—experiences boundless enthusiasm for exploration. This placement is ruled by excessive Jupiter, leading to escapism through blind faith in life's possibilities and an incessant search for the newest horizon that may leave you unsatisfied with what is. Transcendence is achieved through channeling your expansive vision into artistic creativity in order to curb the constant wanderlust.

NEPTUNE IN CAPRICORN

DATES: 1984–1998

Neptune in Capricorn—the sign of restriction, discipline, and hard work—meets the boundary-dissolving energy of Neptune. Ruled by rule-loving Saturn, this placement melds idealistic fantasy with existing structures. There is a tendency to flee from responsibility or confusion you feel around your sense of purpose and life direction. Transcendence is achieved by channeling your inherent creativity into your work, while finding self-confidence in ways that don't require validation from others.

NEPTUNE IN AQUARIUS

DATES: 1998–2012

Neptune in Aquarius—the sign of personal freedom, uniqueness, and humanitarian efforts—finds itself sympathetic and compassionate with humanity almost to a fault. Ruled by both Saturn and Uranus, this placement desires spiritual soul connections with others that cause you to idealize your friendships and associations, leading to weak boundaries. Transcendence is achieved by owning your uniqueness and seeing your inherent value within each group clearly.

NEPTUNE IN PISCES

DATES: 2012–2025

Neptune in its home sign of Pisces is intuitive and idealistic regarding faith, spirituality, and the ability of the collective to heal both psychic and psychological wounds. Naturally empathic, this placement leaves you susceptible to spiritual deception and escapism as you seek transcendence of this physical plane. True cosmic oneness is found through listening to your own intuition above all others.

Working with My Birth Chart: My Neptune

1. What is your Neptune sign?

    ....

2. Which house does your Neptune fall in and which zodiac sign is the natural ruler of that house?

    ....

3. Compare the key words of your Neptune sign and the natural house ruler (page 26). What insights does that provide you?

    ....
    ....
    ....
    ....
    ....

REFLECTION

How has your Neptune placement influenced the way you have experienced idealism, escapism, and self-sabotage? How can you transcend these experiences?

....
....
....
....

PLUTO ♇

KEY WORDS: transformation; power; death/rebirth

The final outer planet and farthest from our Sun is Pluto. Associated with the mythological god of the underworld, Pluto governs the themes of death, birth, and transformation through surrender and annihilation, as well as sexuality, the occult, the psychological subconscious, and all things taboo.

Pluto is no stranger to transformation, having been demoted to dwarf planet in 2006. This is very on-brand for the tiny planet of power. Despite its dwarf status, Pluto plays an important role in astrology as its ecliptic orbit spends anywhere from 12 to 32 years in a particular sign with a retrograde period of about six months, which asks us to reassess our subconscious drives and examine our shadow selves.

Pluto in your birth chart by sign and house will show you where you experience significant transformation through metaphorical death and rebirth in order to show you your true power. Look to Pluto to illuminate where you experience power struggles, crisis, and regeneration. Do not fear the seemingly dark implications of Pluto, since it's also pointing you toward where you experience tremendous willpower and personal growth potential, as well as where you can completely transform yourself by overcoming any circumstance.

PLUTO IN ARIES

DATES: 1823–1853

Pluto in Aries—the Mars-ruled sign of war, aggression, self-appointed authority, and pioneering spirit—finds transformation through asserting personal "will to power" (to quote Pluto in Aries native Friedrich Nietzsche). Breaking free of herd mentality to be the authority of your life leads you through cycles of conflict and power struggles with others in positions of power. This is a strong theme for you in this lifetime. The meaning of true power lies in the altruistic pursuit of your inner strength.

PLUTO IN TAURUS

DATES: 1853–1884

Pluto in Taurus, the Venus-ruled sign of material wealth and sensual pleasure, finds transformation through overcoming self-indulgence and materialism to fill the void. Your journey includes discovering that while you have the power to leverage financial gain, you must first find value in yourself. Learning that the true importance of wealth and personal power comes from within and finding that security inside yourself are both important themes in this lifetime for you.

PLUTO IN GEMINI

DATES: 1884–1914

Pluto in Gemini—the Mercury-ruled sign of communication, mental agility, and transportation—finds transformation through curious experimentation while pursuing power through knowledge. Challenging experiences may arise in the areas of learning and communicating with authority figures. Even your own siblings may test you as your mind seeks truth. Overall, you may find it difficult to trust others. True power comes from your immense mental capacity and ability to be flexible toward life's paradoxes.

PLUTO IN CANCER

DATES: 1914–1939

Pluto in Cancer—the lunar-ruled sign of home, family, and nurturing—finds transformation through transcending traumatic childhood experiences. Repeating patterns from youth will persist until you acknowledge and deal with them. True power is found through doing the deep psychological work to heal and overcome the wounds of the past. Doing this positions you to experience the nurturing home life you are capable of creating in this lifetime; one that exists on the other side of the painful memories.

PLUTO IN LEO

DATES: 1939–1958

Pluto in Leo—the solar-ruled sign of creativity, self-expression, and loyalty—finds transformation through intense experiences involving passionate romantic relationships, personal creativity, dramatic displays, or the approach to child-rearing. You love being the center of attention and have an incredible drive to create and showcase your talents that may lead to challenges with authority and ego clashes. True power comes from sharing the limelight and learning to manage your emotional outbursts.

PLUTO IN VIRGO

DATES: 1959–1972

Pluto in Virgo—the Mercury-ruled sign of health, routine, and service to others—finds transformation through overcoming controlling situations with authority figures or workplace hierarchies. You love being in charge of your own time and how you spend it, to the point of obsession with your work or routine. Sometimes you might even veer off into workaholic tendencies. True power lies in your ability to find work-life balance and taking good care of your physical body without succumbing to perfectionism.

PLUTO IN LIBRA

DATES: 1971–1984

Pluto in Libra, the Venus-ruled sign of balance and equality in relationships, finds transformation through experiencing challenges and power struggles on the road to harmonious partnership. The obsessive nature of Pluto brings intensity, jealousy, and controlling behavior, leading to challenges maintaining relationships out of fear of losing them. True power comes from accepting the light and shadow qualities within yourself and your partners rather than looking like the perfect pair.

PLUTO IN SCORPIO

DATES: 1984–1995

Pluto finds itself at home in Scorpio, ruler of death, sex, transformation, and all things taboo. This placement amplifies Scorpio's naturally mysterious and intense qualities, seeking transformation through extreme experiences related to sexuality, the occult, and the darker aspects of the human experience. You crave depth in everything you do, although you may fear vulnerability and loss of control. True power comes from sharing your transformation and using it to help others.

PLUTO IN SAGITTARIUS

DATES: 1995–2008

Pluto in Sagittarius—the Jupiter-ruled sign of expansion, truth seeking, adventure, and philosophy—finds transformation through exploration of the world to shape your worldview and personal philosophy. You need to experience life firsthand to digest what the world is here to teach you . . . even if that comes with power struggles and chaotic life lessons. True power comes from transcending the need to be obsessively attached to your ideals and opinions.

PLUTO IN CAPRICORN

DATES: 2008–2024

Pluto in Capricorn—the Saturn-ruled sign of responsibility, hard work, and achievement—finds transformation through painful experiences with corruption in places of authority in the home as well as the structures of society. You see what isn't working and strive to meet change head-on. Armed with Pluto's obsessive tendency for transformation, you know the road will be long and tumultuous. True power comes from learning to work within a team rather than as a solitary leader (a.k.a. learning to play well with others).

PLUTO IN AQUARIUS

DATES: 1778–1798; 2024–2044

Pluto in Aquarius—the Saturn and Uranus co-ruled sign of humanitarian efforts, technology, friendships, and group identity—finds transformation through finding your own unique voice among the crowds in terms of social justice issues and fitting in. You may experience intense struggles with friendships and group identity, leading you to question authority and loyalty. True power comes from maintaining your individuality while working in groups committed to progressive innovation for the benefit of society.

PLUTO IN PISCES

DATES: 1798–1823, 2044–2068

Pluto in Pisces, the Jupiter and Neptune co-ruled sign of spirituality and the subconscious, finds transformation through artistic interpretation as a means of self-healing. Following the tactile efforts of previous generations, obsessive Pluto in intuitive Pisces seeks to understand why we need to feel powerful. This may come through challenging experiences with escapism, substance abuse, and feeling victimized to find the meaning of true power through facing fears and psychological healing.

Working with My Birth Chart: My Pluto

1. What is your Pluto sign?

    ....

2. Which house does your Pluto fall in and which zodiac sign is the natural ruler of that house?

    ....

3. Compare the key words of your Pluto sign and the natural house ruler (page 26). What insights does that provide you?

    ....

    ....

    ....

    ....

    ....

REFLECTION

Notice how your Pluto placement affects how you experience power struggles, conflict, and crisis. How can you transform yourself based on these experiences and discover your personal power?

....

....

....

....

Planetary Symbols

Match the planetary symbol or glyph with its corresponding planet.

☉	MERCURY
☿	VENUS
♅	MARS
♄	JUPITER
♇	SATURN
☽	URANUS
♃	NEPTUNE
♀	PLUTO
♆	SUN
♂	MOON

Zodiac Symbols

Match the Zodiac symbol or glyph with it's corresponding name.

⧎   ARIES

♌   TAURUS

♋   GEMINI

♌   CANCER

♏   LEO

♎   VIRGO

♓   LIBRA

♒   SCORPIO

♉   SAGITTARIUS

♈   CAPRICORN

♍   AQUARIUS

♐   PISCES

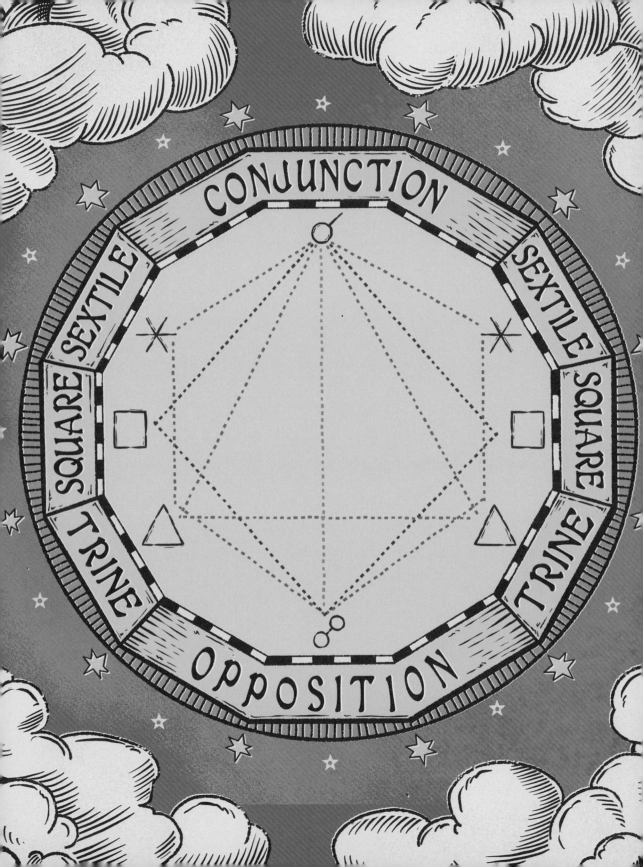

NINE

Learning about the Aspects

· · · · · · · · · · · · · · · · · ·

WHEN WE LOOK at the stars at night, everything may appear stationary, but the planets are always moving around, sliding from one house to another. In the astrological world, this means they're forming aspects, which can affect the energy of the day. Aspects are mathematical calculations that measure the distance between planets to reveal their relationship, as if they are speaking to one another from different parts of the sky within your chart.

In astrology, the relationship between two or more planets in your birth chart are represented by the lines you'll see making zigzagging across the zodiac wheel. Each of these lines represents the three basic types of aspects: harmonious, challenging, and conjunctions. These aspects reveal areas of your chart by planet, sign, and house that create tension or motivation, or show areas of ease and merging energy.

Learning to read the aspect grid in your chart will help you understand the lines of communication between the planets, leading to a deeper understanding of your personality. Knowing your aspects is incredibly helpful in overcoming patterns and behaviors that may hinder your progress and help you to cultivate self-compassion. It also shows you where you shine naturally so you can optimize that energy to your benefit.

Aspects are nuanced and complex. There are entire books written about them, and astrologers can spend many hours pondering their meaning in a single birth chart. Since this workbook is meant to be introductory, I want to give you enough information to spark your curiosity. If you are intrigued by the aspects, I have a list of astrology resources (see page 182) that can help you learn more.

THE ASPECT GRID

The aspect grid is located beneath the natal chart. It often looks like a staircase of boxes containing all of the planetary glyphs and aspect symbols, connected to another box that lists the planets next to the sign and degree of your natal planets.

The planets go in order, beginning with the Sun. Using your finger, you can trace down each individual column and see which aspect symbols appear, then follow that column to the right to see which planet it is aspecting. Most astrology websites generate the harmonious aspects in blue, while challenging aspects are shown in red. This corresponds to the color of the lines on your natal chart.

HARMONIOUS ASPECTS

The two most important harmonious aspects found in your natal chart are sextiles and trines. You will recognize them by their symbols ✶ for sextile and △ for trine on the aspect grid at the bottom of your chart.

SEXTILE 60° ✶

The pie piece for each house in the zodiac is 30 degrees. This means that planets that are two signs/houses away from one another are 60 degrees apart, a relationship known as a sextile. A sextile in your chart represents ease or an opportunity that may come in the form of helpful people in your life. The opportunity will depend on the planets involved.

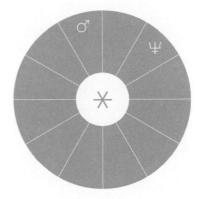

For example, a sextile between your Sun and Moon will show harmony between your feelings and how you express yourself, creating opportunities to shine (Sun) when tapping into your emotions and intuition (Moon).

TRINE 120° △

Planets that are four signs/houses away from one another, or 120 degrees apart, are categorized as a trine. A trine in your birth chart shows an area of ease and flow. When two or more planets form a trine with one another, they are experiencing the same elemental energy—earth, air, fire, or water—leading them to understand one another clearly.

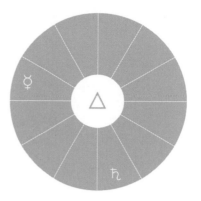

For example, Venus trine Jupiter can present good fortune in relationships, making you optimistic, inspiring, and loving. Trines can also show you where you are lazy and might benefit from putting more effort into capitalizing on these auspicious aspects.

Working with My Birth Chart: Sextiles and Trines

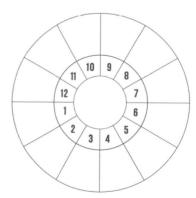

1. Fill in the zodiac wheel with your planetary placements, then locate the sextiles and trines by calculating the distance between the planets by counting houses.

2. Draw different types of lines between the planets to represent each sextile and trine.

REFLECTION

Think of a time you benefited from the harmonious aspects in your chart. How can you bring more fortunate energy into your life based on these aspects?

....

....

....

....

CHALLENGING ASPECTS

The two most important challenging aspects found in your natal chart are squares and oppositions. You will recognize them by their symbols □ for square and ☍ for opposition on the aspect grid at the bottom of your chart.

SQUARE 90° □

Planets that are three signs/houses away from one another, or 90 degrees apart, are known as a square. Squares in your natal chart create tension, as if the two planets were rubbing together, creating uncomfortable internal friction. This type of tension creates the need for change to alleviate the pressure. While squares aren't fun, they are necessary to help you grow and evolve in the areas represented by the planets involved.

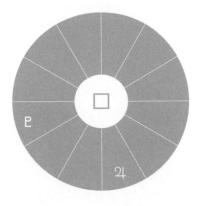

For example, a square between your Sun and Moon can feel like a constant struggle between allowing your personality to shine (Sun) and feeling emotionally safe (Moon) in doing so. Creating your own sense of inner safety will lead to more confidence in being seen.

OPPOSITION 180° ☍

Planets that are six signs/houses away from one another, or 180 degrees apart, are known as oppositions. Planets in opposition are directly across the sky from one another, literally opposing the energy of the other, creating friction. Consider the planets involved, staring each other down from across the sky, both refusing to relent in their energy.

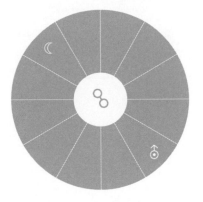

For example, if you have your Sun opposite your Moon in your birth chart, you were born on a full Moon, and your core personality (Sun) is opposing your emotional needs (Moon), creating competition that requires constant compromise on your part.

While seemingly frustrating, learning to compromise will show you how to tap into the resources of both planets.

Working with My Birth Chart: Squares and Oppositions

1. Fill in the zodiac wheel with your planetary placements, then locate the squares and oppositions by calculating the distance between the planets by counting houses.

2. Draw different types of lines between the planets to represent each square and opposition.

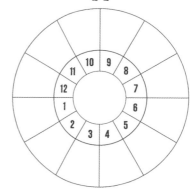

REFLECTION

How has the discovery of challenging aspects in your birth chart shown you where you can experience growth?

....

....

....

....

CONJUNCTIONS 0° ☌

Planets that appear in the same house/sign as another planet within 3 degrees in either direction are known as conjunctions. You will recognize them by the ☌ symbol in the aspect grid at the bottom of your chart. This aspect is neither challenging nor beneficial by its nature; instead, it depends on the planets involved.

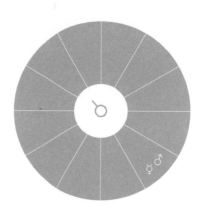

Conjunctions are significant when they show up in your birth chart. When two or more planets form a conjunction, they are blending their energies. They gain strength as a unit but lose the potency of their individuality, just like blending ingredients in a recipe. For example, if your Sun is conjunct your Moon, you were born on a new Moon, which is the strongest merging of these two important celestial bodies. This conjunction aligns your personality and wants (Sun) with your emotional needs (Moon), making you incredibly strong, decisive, and independent.

Working with My Birth Chart: Conjunctions

1. Fill in the zodiac wheel with your planetary place-ments, then locate the conjunctions in your chart by finding the planets that share one house.

2. Draw a circle around the planets that are conjunct.

REFLECTION

In what areas of your life might your conjunctions bring you strength? What traits can these merged planetary energies bring out in your personality?

....

....

....

....

ASPECT PATTERNS

In addition to the five major aspects, there are three important aspect patterns that can appear in your birth chart: grand trines, T-squares, and grand crosses. Each of these aspect patterns is made up of a combination of aspects and plays an important role in your personality in this lifetime.

GRAND TRINE

A grand trine is an aspect pattern formed by three trines in your birth chart that come together in a particular element (earth, air, fire, or water). Trines are harmonious aspects in your chart, indicating something that comes easily and naturally to you. Looking at the three planets involved in a grand trine will show you the beneficial energy that occurs when these three planets connect. It's important to nurture this aspect pattern to maximize its benefits over your lifetime.

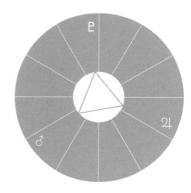

T-SQUARE

The T-square is an aspect pattern formed when two or more planets oppose one another and also form a square to another planet or planets, making a literal T shape in your birth chart. Squares and oppositions are challenging aspects that require effort and attention in order to promote growth and integration. The planet that forms the square is where you find the energy to bring balance to the tension created by the planets in opposition.

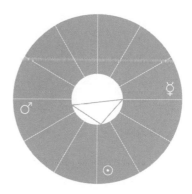

GRAND CROSS

A grand cross is an aspect pattern formed when two different sets of planets in opposition cross one another in the sky. Oppositions are challenging aspects, and with the presence of two opposing oppositions, you can experience many challenges along the road of life that require you to be present, focused, and aware to bring balance to the planets involved in the grand cross.

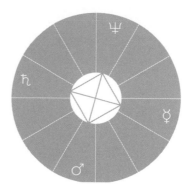

Working with My Birth Chart: Aspect Patterns

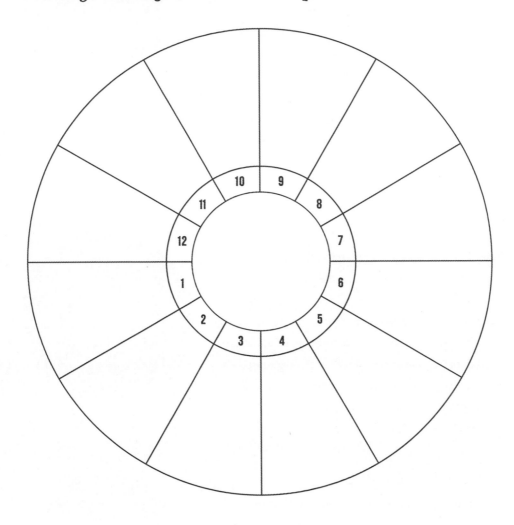

1. Looking at your own birth chart, place a small dot to represent each planet in your chart that forms one of the major aspect patterns onto the zodiac wheel.

2. Draw different lines to show the grand trine, grand cross, or T-square patterns.

3. In my birth chart, I see the following aspect pattern(s):

    ....

4. These aspect patterns can be interpreted to mean:

    ....

    ....

REFLECTION

Knowing now that particular aspect pattern(s) exist in your chart, how do you think you can harness the energy of the planets involved in order to maximize your potential in this lifetime?

....

....

....

....

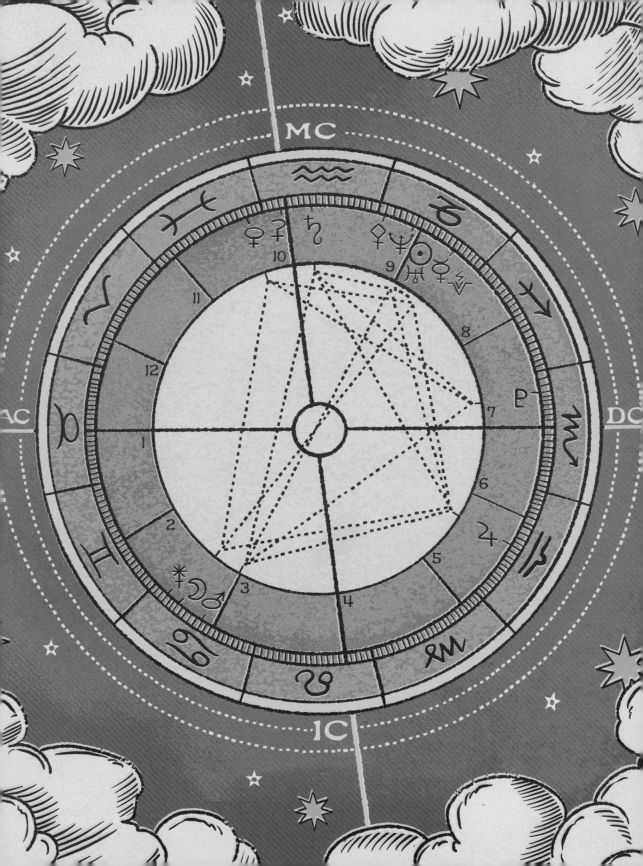

TEN

Digging Deeper into Your Birth Chart

· · · · · · · · · · · · · · · · · · · ·

ANALYZING YOUR BIRTH chart is the gift that keeps on giving. It takes time to understand and integrate the many layers and nuances of your personal astrology, which means you can scratch the surface one day and dive as deep as you like on another. Once you have a general understanding of your planetary placements and their energies along with the houses and aspects, you can move on to discover even more layers to your chart. The more you study, the more you'll learn about yourself.

The following chapter takes an introductory look at other planetary bodies and points in your chart that play a significant role in your personality and life path. This includes asteroids, which are not as important as the major planets, but are notable in their subtle energetic effects. We will also touch upon the importance of the lunar nodes and the four major chart points MC, IC, AC, and DC, which help you develop over the course of your lifetime. We will also look at the actual shape of your chart, the patterns your planets form, and where they are located, which all play an important role in understanding who you are and what you are meant to do in this lifetime. Finally, we'll look at planet retrogrades as well as the strength or weakness of your planetary placements as categorized by the four dignities.

ASTEROIDS

Asteroids are minor planets that are associated with Greek and Roman mythology. There are over 12,000 documented asteroids in our solar system, which can be researched on any number of free astrology websites while calculating your birth chart. Don't get too overwhelmed, though! In astrology we tend to focus on the following five asteroids specifically. Using your knowledge of what each sign and house represents will show you what each asteroid represents in your birth chart.

CHIRON ⚷

Chiron is categorized as an asteroid, although it is actually a comet! Known as the wounded healer, it's mythologically represented by a centaur who was wounded by an arrow and could not fully heal. In your natal chart, your Chiron placement by house and sign will show you the unhealed wound you carry in this lifetime. By working toward healing yourself, you become available to teach others how to heal.

CERES ⚳

Ceres is the asteroid that represents cycles of growth, nourishment, and nurturing that is mythologically connected to Demeter, goddess of the harvest and mother to Persephone. Your Ceres placement by house and sign will show you how you mother yourself, which includes how you feed and nurture yourself and others.

PALLAS ⚴

Pallas is the asteroid that represents wisdom and the inner warrior of feminine energy. Mythologically connected to Pallas Athena, wise warrior daughter of Zeus, your Pallas placement by house and sign will show you how you strategically approach conflict from a place of knowledge rather than brute force.

JUNO ⚵

Juno is the asteroid that represents the light and dark sides of marriage or long-term, committed partnerships. It is mythologically connected to Hera, loyal wife of unfaithful

Zeus. Your Juno sign will show you what attracts and drives you in relationships, along with your wounds connected to attachment.

VESTA ⚶

Vesta is the asteroid associated with the proverbial temples we build and tend, our home and hearth. Mythologically connected to the vestal virgins who tended the sacred flame, your Vesta placement by house and sign will show you where you create sacred spaces of devotion and how you serve them.

Working with My Birth Chart: Asteroids

1. List the five asteroids and which houses they appear in on your chart.

   ....

   ....

2. Which asteroids appear in the same signs or houses as your other planets?

   ....

   ....

3. Note if any asteroids occupy houses or signs that were previously empty. List them.

   ....

   ....

REFLECTION

How do you feel the energy of your asteroid placements plays a role in your personality?

....

....

....

....

LUNAR NODES ☊ ☋

The lunar nodes are two points where the Sun and Moon meet up during the eclipses that are associated with destiny, fate, and past lives. Opposing one another from across the heavens, the North Node and South Node are cosmically connected to where you are going and where you came from. The house and sign that your North Node (also called your "True Node") is stationed in will help you to understand the qualities and motivations around your greater purpose. Your North Node will challenge you; it will feel unfamiliar and uncomfortable, where as your South Node will feel easy and safe. Taking the path of ease will not bring you the growth and satisfaction you desire in this lifetime, while following your North Node will bring auspicious opportunities and incredible fulfillment.

DOMINANT HOUSES

The zodiac wheel can be broken up into three types of houses, known as angular, succedent, and cadent houses. The house type where most of your planets reside is known as your dominant house type. It's normal to have planets in two or all three types rather than just one. Any house that contains a planet has extra importance in your life, while empty houses are still impactful, just less significant.

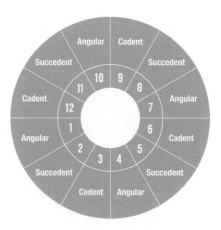

ANGULAR HOUSES—1, 4, 7, 10

The angular houses in your birth chart are known for being action-oriented houses, since they are associated with the Cardinal signs Aries, Cancer, Libra, and Capricorn. If several of your natal planets fall in these houses, you are an angular-dominant person, known for initiating, taking the lead, and getting things started.

SUCCEDENT HOUSES—2, 5, 8, 11

The succedent houses in your birth chart are known for being grounded and stable, since they are associated with the Fixed signs Taurus, Leo, Scorpio, and Aquarius. If several of your natal planets fall in these houses, you are a succedent-dominant person, known for your steady, reliable personality. You commit wholeheartedly, knowing how to get things done.

CADENT HOUSES—3,6,9,12

The cadent houses in your birth chart are known for being flexible and adaptable, since they are associated with the Mutable signs Gemini, Virgo, Sagittarius, and Pisces. If several of your natal planets fall in these houses, you are a cadent-dominant person, known for going with the flow, being open to change, and constantly in motion.

Working with My Birth Chart: Dominant Houses

1. List the houses containing most of your planets, noting if they are angular, succedent, or cadent.

   ....

   ....

2. Which houses are empty? Note whether they are angular, succedent, or cadent.

   ....

   ....

3. How do you feel the houses that contain the majority of your planets might play a role in your personality?

   ....

   ....

REFLECTION

How do you feel about the significance of the empty houses in your birth chart?

....

....

THE AC-DC AND MC-IC AXES

You will notice the initials AC, DC, MC, and IC on your chart. These important points are the cusps of the four angular houses, known as the AC-DC and MC-IC axes. We refer to these points as an axis because they are in direct opposition to one another. These four sensitive points are activated through planetary aspects and transits and will show you where you've come from and where you are going.

Your AC, or Ascendant, describes how the world perceives you at first blush as well as your connection to your First House, which opposes your Seventh House cusp. Your DC, or Descendent, describes what you seek in relationships. The AC-DC axis describes the relationship between the self and others. For example, a Cancer AC will be incredibly emotional and nurturing, a quality easily shown to the world and something others seek in you, while the opposing Capricorn highlights the structure and stability you seek in your relationships to help ground your strong emotions.

The MC-IC axis relates to who you are at home versus who you are out in the world. The IC (Imum Coeli), located on the cusp of the Fourth House, represents your private psychological world and home life. Opposite your IC on the cusp of your Tenth House is your very public MC (Medium Coeli, or Midheaven), which describes your professional life and social status. We need work-life balance in order to create the life that suits our individual tastes and desires. Knowing your core needs for family and home life—as described by your IC—will help you tap into the confidence you need to seek the environ-ments and resources described by your MC when you are in the public eye, creating a legacy and engaging in meaningful work. For example, a Leo IC will want a creative, joyful home base where they feel seen by loved ones so they can go out into the world and be their Aquarius self, who doesn't need that individual recognition and validation. They are team players who put the group needs before their own.

HEMISPHERES

The zodiac wheel is broken up into four hemispheres, Southern, Northern, Eastern, and Western. However, the placement of these hemispheres is backward compared to what we are used to seeing when looking at a globe! The hemispheres that contain the major-ity of your planets describe the energy of your chart.

SOUTHERN

The Southern Hemisphere is located above the AC/DC axis and contains Houses 7–12, including the MC or Midheaven. This hemisphere is associated with the conscious realm, and planets located in the Southern Hemisphere are considered more extroverted or in the public eye.

NORTHERN

The Northern Hemisphere is located beneath the AC/DC axis and contains Houses 1–6, including the IC or Imum Coeli. This hemisphere is associated with the unconscious realm, and planets located in the Northern Hemisphere are considered to be more introverted or involved in their own inner process.

EASTERN

The Eastern Hemisphere is located to the left of the MC/IC axis and contains Houses 1–3 and 10–12, and includes the AC, or Ascendant. This hemisphere is associated with the self, placing the emphasis on your own sense of independence and following your inner direction.

WESTERN

The Western Hemisphere is located to the right of the MC/IC axis and contains Houses 4–9, including the DC, or Descendent. This hemisphere is associated with other people in your life, placing the emphasis on the interactions and relationships you have with others.

PATTERNS

Another factor to consider when interpreting your birth chart is the display pattern your planets make. In the late 1800s, astrologer Marc Edmund Jones identified seven chart patterns by observing just two factors: the directions and shapes the patterns made (without considering the houses or axes). Look at your own chart and see which of the following patterns it makes and how that shapes your own energy.

BOWL

The bowl-shaped chart indicates that all of your planets are concentrated on one side of your chart, with most of the houses empty on the other side. This is easily recognized by an opposition of 180 degrees between the first and last planet in the pattern. This pattern indicates a self-contained personality that needs to learn to integrate the opposite side of your chart.

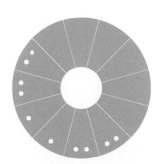

BUCKET

The bucket-shaped chart is very similar to the bowl, however one planet is on the opposite side of the chart, forming the so-called "handle" of the bucket. This metaphorical planetary handle is carrying the rest of the chart, indicating a strong emphasis on that particular planet as it helps you strive to share your uniqueness.

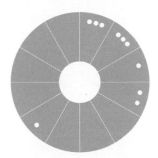

BUNDLE

A bundle may look similar to a bowl, however the bundle-shaped chart has all planets contained within four houses or a 120-degree trine while the rest of the houses remain empty. This pattern indicates a hyperfocused personality that is driven to succeed. Balance with the empty houses is needed for a fully integrated personality.

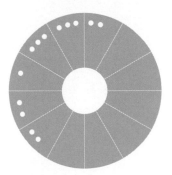

FAN

The fan-shaped chart is similar to the bucket, where there is one planet that forms a handle that is opposite the rest of the planets in the bundle shape of a 120-degree trine. This pattern indicates that the drive and ambition of the bundle is channeled through the planet(s) that oppose the rest of the chart.

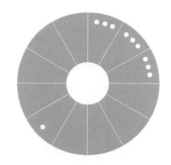

LOCOMOTIVE

The locomotive-shaped chart has all planets contained within 240 degrees of the chart, leaving a trine, or 120 degrees, empty. Following the planets clockwise will show the locomotive drive of the individual by noticing which planet is driving the train. This pattern indicates a strong will to move forward and achieve success.

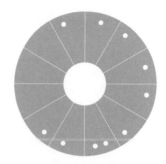

SEESAW

The seesaw-shaped chart has two significant opposing groups of planets on either side of the chart, leaving at least two houses—or 60 degrees—empty on either side. This pattern indicates a challenge to integrate two very different sides of one's personality, often needing to express both before reaching balance.

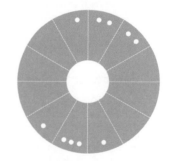

SPLASH

The splash-shaped chart doesn't seem to follow any of the other patterns, with planets spread out throughout at least seven of the houses. This pattern indicates a rich and diverse personality with many widespread interests. However, there may be challenges caused by feeling energetically scattered and struggling to find focus.

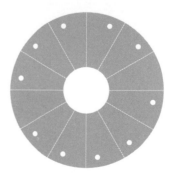

SPLAY

The splay chart can resemble a tripod shape, with three clusters of planets broken up by empty houses. This pattern indicates a multitalented individual who values their independence. There is also a need for integration between unrelated skill sets in order to maximize your potential.

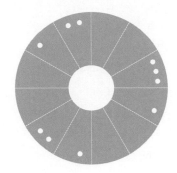

Working with My Birth Chart: Patterns

1. Looking at your own birth chart, place a small dot to represent each planet in your chart on the zodiac wheel.

2. The pattern of my planets most closely matches:

    ☐ bowl   ☐ seesaw
    ☐ bundle   ☐ bucket
    ☐ fan   ☐ splash
    ☐ locomotive   ☐ splay

    This pattern can be interpreted as

    ....

3. Most of my planets appear in the hemisphere:

    ☐ Southern   ☐ Northern   ☐ Eastern   ☐ Western

    This can be interpreted as

    ....

REFLECTION

How do you feel your chart pattern and hemisphere placement of your birth chart affect your personality or how you take action in your life?

....

....

THE FOUR DIGNITIES

When a planet is positioned in a particular sign in your birth chart, that position can affect the strength or weakness of that planet. In other words, each planet in your chart will still have an effect on you, but the potency varies due to planetary rulership—and that rulership is categorized in the following four dignities:

- Domiciles are the home position of a sign.
- Detriments are the opposite of the home position of a sign.
- Exaltations are a position of peak awareness, where a sign may achieve its most potent energy.
- Falls are the opposite of the exaltation of a sign.

For example, since Mars is ruled by Aries, its dignity is in its Domicile when it appears in Aries in a birth chart. Mars is weakest, or Detriment, when in the opposite sign to Aries, which is Libra. Mars will achieve its most potent energy when it's in the dignity of Exaltation, in Capricorn. It will be weakest in energy when it falls in Capricorn's opposite, Cancer.

Try not to feel discouraged if one of your planets is in its Detriment or Fall position. My Scorpio Moon and Libra Mars are in their weakest possible positions, and I have never let that hold me back. Even the weakest planetary placements hold powerful meaning for you. Plus, you have many other important placements in your birth chart to support your many strengths! You will notice that only the seven planets that are visible to the naked eye are historically categorized in their Exaltation and Fall positions. Know that the dignities aren't something to stress about! All of your signs have an effect on you, whether they have their full power or are operating from a weaker position. For example, your Ascendant sign is powerful regardless of its dignity.

Working with My Birth Chart: Dignities

The table below illustrates each sign at its peak powerfulness and its opposite, or weakest, position. Fill in your signs and then review the chart, circling if your sign is placed as a dignity.

PLANET	MY PLACEMENTS	DOMICILE	DETRIMENT	EXALTATION	FALL
SUN		Leo	Aquarius	Aries	Libra
MOON		Cancer	Capricorn	Taurus	Scorpio
MERCURY		Gemini, Virgo	Sagittarius, Pisces	Virgo	Pisces
VENUS		Taurus, Libra	Scorpio, Aries	Pisces	Virgo
MARS		Aries	Libra	Capricorn	Cancer
JUPITER		Sagittarius	Gemini	Cancer	Capricorn
SATURN		Capricorn	Cancer	Libra	Aries
URANUS		Aquarius	Leo	....	....
NEPTUNE		Pisces	Virgo	....	....
PLUTO		Scorpio	Taurus	....	....

RETROGRADES

Retrogrades are nothing to fear! Except for the Sun, Moon, and Earth, every planet experiences its own retrograde period. A retrograde motion occurs when our view of the planet from Earth appears to slow down, stop, and move backward along the ecliptic. The closer the planet is to the Sun, the more often this will happen. Mercury is the most frequent offender, experiencing its retrograde cycle three to four times a year, while Venus and Mars only experience retrogrades every one and a half to two years. The remaining social and outer planets actually spend up to half a year in retrograde annually, but their effects are more subtle due to their distance from the Sun.

So what does that mean, and should you be worried? Nope! Throughout astrology, as in life, there are periods when action feels natural and other periods where you may feel called to rest and go inward. Consider each retrograde as a period of inner reflection; a time to recharge, reset, and course-correct before the next wave of action. The planet experiencing the retrograde will offer clues to the area of life most affected, showing you where to slow down and how to look within.

Working with My Birth Chart: Retrogrades

1. Look at your chart for the retrograde symbol (lowercase *r* next to the planetary glyph).

2. How many planets were in retrograde? Which ones?

   ....

3. What areas of your life do these planets influence?

   ....
   ....

REFLECTION

How do you feel the retrograde planets in your chart have affected your life as they correspond to the themes of that planet's energy or the house they reside in? (To interpret these planets, consider the energy of the planet affecting you internally rather than externally—meaning they are expressed inwardly or privately rather than outwardly.) Or, if there are no retrograde planets in your chart, how do you feel retrograde transit periods affect you?

....
....
....

Appendix

Sample Charts

·······························

Beyoncé

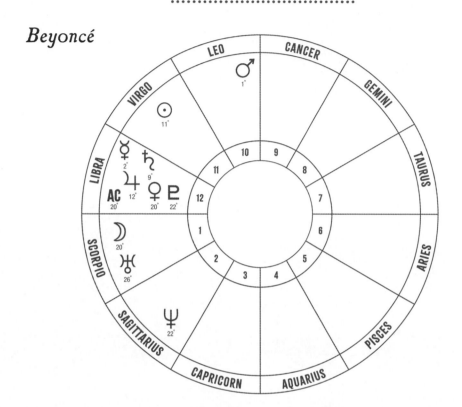

Beyoncé is a feminist singer-songwriter and actress known for the inspiring, empowering messages within her music and her innovative artistry. She was born September 4, 1981, in Houston, Texas, at 10:00 a.m., making her a Virgo Sun, Scorpio Moon, Libra Ascendant. Beautiful, artistic Venus is her chart ruler, supported by her hardworking Virgo Sun. The bowl shape of her chart indicates her fierce independence and drive to succeed. With transformative Pluto conjunct her Ascendant, she radiates power that translates through the lens of fair, balanced Libra. Her Scorpio Moon in her Second House makes a harmonious trine to her Midheaven, supporting the emotional need to bring her values to her legacy. The concentration of planets in Libra along with her prominently featured Pluto and Pluto-ruled Moon help transform the Venusian influence of pure aesthetics into something potent and impactful, a true force to be reckoned with.

Frida Kahlo

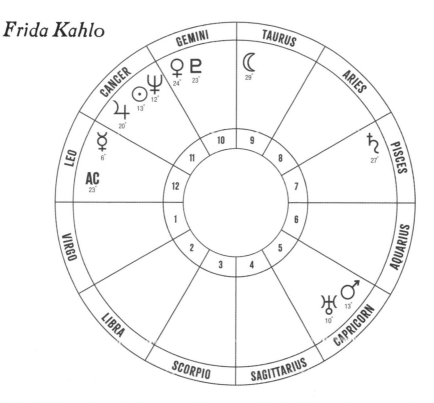

Frida Kahlo was born in Coyoacán, Mexico, on July 6, 1907, at 8:30 a.m., making her a Cancer Sun, Taurus Moon, Leo Ascendant. Her Cancer Sun was conjunct Neptune along with Jupiter in her Eleventh House of friendships and group association, and she was known for being active in the Communist party as well as being married to political muralist Diego Rivera. With artistic Venus conjunct powerful, intense Pluto in communicative, mutable Gemini also in her Eleventh House, she transmuted her pain and suffering connected with passion, love, and pleasure through her paintings. Her Leo rising is connected to her iconic style, and she expressed her individuality and emotions through her work and lifestyle, as echoed by her Taurus Moon at 29 degrees (a Leo degree, an indicator of fame in a birth chart), in weak conjunction with her Midheaven. Oppositions from unpredictable Uranus conjunct volatile Mars to her Sun, indicating pain and upheaval; however, she was meant to make an impact on the world by sharing her trauma through her art.

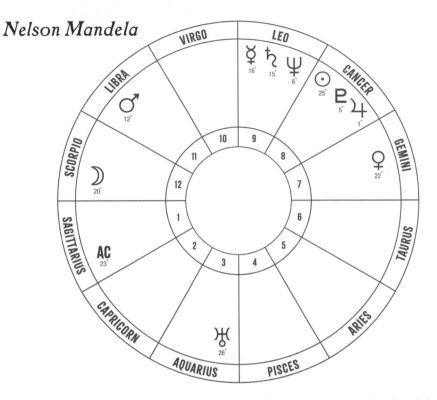

Nelson Mandela

Nelson Mandela was a South African anti-apartheid activist who helped end the country's system of racial segregation. He later became the nation's first democratically elected leader and received the Nobel Peace Prize for his role in creating a peaceful transfer of power. He was born on July 18, 1918, in Mvezo, South Africa, at 2:54 p.m., making him a Cancer Sun, Scorpio Moon, Sagittarius Ascendant. Jupiter, his chart ruler, was positioned opposite his Ascendant sign, creating interpersonal challenges while on the path of seeking truth. Mandela was famously incarcerated for more than 27 years, and emotionally intelligent Scorpio Moon in his Twelfth House of imprisonment and isolation demonstrates his capacity to endure long periods of seclusion. His Uranus in humanitarian Aquarius sits in his Third House of communication, weakly opposing his Virgo Midheaven, which shows great change and upheaval challenging his legacy of selfless service. Mercury conjunct Saturn in performative Leo tempers the enthusiastic expression of Mercury, indicating his concentrated focus on communicating what was of greatest importance to and benefit for society.

Prince

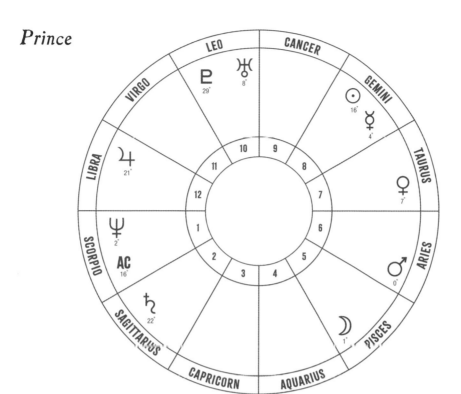

The musician Prince was born in Minneapolis, Minnesota, on June 7, 1958, at 6:17 p.m., making him a Gemini Sun, Pisces Moon, Scorpio Ascendant. His mutable Sun and Moon are the perfect combination of Gemini's prolific wordsmithing and vocal affinity with Pisces's musical artistry. His intense Scorpio rising gave him the look of mysterious, sexy glamour and the talent to back it up. His Pluto at 29 degrees Leo conjunct with his 29 degree Leo Midheaven are indicators of fame through transforming the taboo, a hallmark of his boundary-pushing performances and overall presence. Having several planets in mutable signs (Sun, Moon, Mercury, and Saturn) are clues to his evolving identity, changing his name from Prince to a symbol (which appeared to be a blend of the Mars and Venus glyphs) to create something that transcended gender. He was later referred to as the Artist Formerly Known as Prince, and the Artist. Despite his fame, his Pisces Moon in his Fourth House opposing Pluto and his MC caused a push-and-pull between his very public persona and protecting his private life.

Your Birth Chart

Fill in your birth chart below using all you've learned throughout this book. Then, fill in your details on the next page.

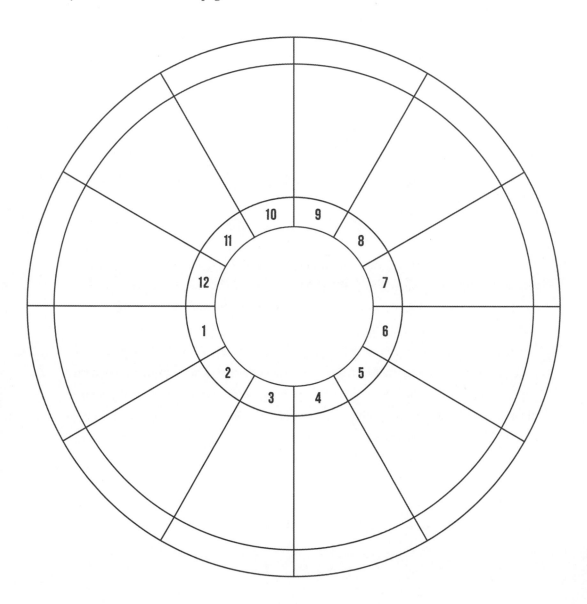

My Sun is in the .... House, in the sign of .... at .... degrees.

My Moon is in the .... House, in the sign of .... at .... degrees.

My Ascendant sign is in the .... House, in the sign of .... at .... degrees.

My Mercury is in the .... House, in the sign of .... at .... degrees.

My Venus is in the .... House, in the sign of .... at .... degrees.

My Mars is in the .... House, in the sign of .... at .... degrees.

My Jupiter is in the .... House, in the sign of .... at .... degrees.

My Saturn is in the .... House, in the sign of .... at .... degrees.

My Uranus is in the .... House, in the sign of .... at .... degrees.

My Neptune is in the .... House, in the sign of .... at .... degrees.

My Pluto is in the .... House, in the sign of .... at .... degrees.

Additional notes: ....

....

....

....

....

....

....

....

....

NOTES

NOTES

NOTES

....
....
....
....
....
....
....
....
....
....
....
....
....
....
....
....
....
....
....
....
....
....
....
....

NOTES

Glossary

....

AQUARIUS: The eleventh sign of the zodiac and natural ruler of the Eleventh House. Classical ruler Saturn, modern ruler Uranus.

ARIES: The first sign of the zodiac and natural ruler of the First House, ruled by Mars.

ASCENDANT (AC): Cusp of the First House of the birth chart, representing one's physical attributes and first impressions.

ASPECT: The angle planets make to one another, along with major points in the birth chart.

ASTEROID: A small celestial body. Asteroids are categorized as minor planets found in our solar system orbiting the Sun.

ASTROLOGY: The study of the movements and relative positions of celestial bodies, interpreted as having an influence on human affairs and the natural world.

BIRTH/NATAL CHART: A map showing the positions of the planets at the time of someone's birth, from which astrologers are said to be able to deduce character or potential.

CANCER: The fourth sign in astrology and natural ruler of the Fourth House, ruled by the Moon.

CAPRICORN: The tenth sign in astrology and natural ruler of the Tenth House, ruled by Saturn.

CERES: Asteroid of nurturance and cycles, associated with Demeter, mother of Persephone.

CHIRON: Wounded Healer asteroid associated with the centaur who was mortally wounded, actually a comet.

CONJUNCTION: Two or more planets in the same house or sign within 0–3 degrees of each other, blending their energy.

DESCENDANT (DC): Cusp of the Seventh House of the birth chart, describes the other people in one's life, qualities they seek in partnership of all kinds.

DUALITIES: The expression of a sign in terms of masculine/feminine energy as pertaining to outward- or inward-directed energy, not gendered.

ECLIPTIC: Imaginary line on the sky marking the path of the Sun, also followed by the Moon and planets.

ELEMENTS: Pertaining to the four elements of the signs in astrology, earth, air, fire, and water.

GEMINI: The third sign in astrology and natural ruler of the Third House. Ruled by Mercury.

HOUSES: The 12 areas in astrology that each describe a different facet of life.

IMUM COELI (IC): Cusp of the Fourth House, describes the home environment and parts of oneself kept private.

INNER PLANETS: The three planets closest to the Sun—Mercury, Venus, and Mars—that have the most personal impact on a person.

JUNO: Marriage asteroid associated with Hera, faithful wife of Zeus.

JUPITER: Categorized as a social planet, Jupiter is the planet of luck, expansion, spirituality, and truth.

LEO: The fifth sign of the zodiac and natural ruler of the Fifth House. Ruled by the Sun.

LIBRA: The seventh sign of the zodiac and natural ruler of the Seventh House. Ruled by Venus.

LUNAR NODES: North and South Nodes of the Moon, associated with destiny and past-life karma.

MARS: Categorized as an inner planet, Mars is the planet of aggression, desire, and assertion.

MEDIUM COELI/MIDHEAVEN (MC): The cusp of the Tenth House; describes the career, legacy, and work in the public.

MERCURY: Categorized as an inner planet, Mercury is the planet of communication and the mind.

MODALITY: Describes the energetic movement of a sign. There are three modalities: cardinal, fixed, and mutable.

MOON: One of the two luminaries in astrology, representing one's emotions, intuition, and private self.

NEPTUNE: Categorized as an outer planet, Neptune is the planet of illusion, dreams, creativity, spirituality, deception, and escapism.

OPPOSITION: Challenging aspect where two or more planets are 180 degrees apart, opposing one another in the birth chart and creating tension.

OUTER PLANETS: Planets farthest from the Sun: Uranus, Neptune, and Pluto. Due to their lengthy orbits, they have a greater impact on groups of people and are known as generational planets.

PALLAS: Asteroid associated with wisdom and strategy, attributed to warrior goddess Athena, daughter of Zeus.

PISCES: The twelfth sign of the zodiac and natural ruler of the Twelfth House. Classical ruler Jupiter, modern ruler Neptune.

PLANET: Celestial body orbiting the Sun in our solar system. In astrology, each planet is assigned particular character attributes that affect each person within their unique birth chart.

PLUTO: Categorized as an outer planet, Pluto is the planet of power, destruction, surrender, transformation, all things taboo, and the occult.

QUADRUPLICITIES: The state or fact of being quadruple or fourfold. In astrology, the zodiac is divided into three groups of four signs: the cardinal signs, the fixed signs, and the mutable signs, with each sign separated from the next nearest within the group by 90 degrees of the ecliptic.

RETROGRADE: The apparent backward planetary motion visible from Earth.

SAGITTARIUS: The ninth sign in the zodiac and natural ruler of the Ninth House. Ruled by Jupiter.

SCORPIO: The eighth sign in the zodiac and natural ruler of the Eighth House. Classical ruler Mars, modern ruler Pluto.

SEXTILE: Harmonious aspect where two or more planets are 60 degrees or two signs apart in the birth chart, creating opportunities and beneficial meetings with others.

SOCIAL PLANETS: Jupiter and Saturn, slower moving than inner planets, have an effect on society as well as personally within the birth chart.

SQUARE: Challenging aspect where two or more planets are 90 degrees or three signs apart in the birth chart, creating tension.

SUN: Brightest luminary in the zodiac; represents one's ego and core personality.

TAURUS: The second sign in the zodiac and natural ruler of the Second House. Ruled by Venus.

TRINE: Harmonious aspect where two or more planets are 120 degrees or four signs apart in the birth chart, indicating ease and flow between the planets involved.

VENUS: Categorized as an inner planet, Venus is the planet of love, beauty, harmony, and money.

VESTA: Asteroid and keeper of our spiritual flame, associated with the mythological Vestal virgins.

VIRGO: Sixth sign of the zodiac and natural ruler of the Sixth House. Ruled by Mercury.

ZODIAC: An imaginary belt of the heavens, extending about 8 degrees on each side of the ecliptic, within which lie the visible paths of the Sun, Moon, and principal planets. It contains 12 constellations, and hence 12 divisions known as the signs of the zodiac.

Resources

....

ASTROLOGY ONLINE

www.astrologyhub.com
A one-stop shop for reputable courses and resources, including a podcast featuring top astrological contributors.

www.thedarkpixieastrology.com
Founded by astrologer and author Nic Gaudetter, Dark Pixie boasts one of the most comprehensive free archives of easy-to-understand astrology articles and affordable digital classes.

www.lovelanyadoo.com
The mecca for weekly horoscopes and podcasts from author, humanistic astrologer, and psychic medium Jessica Lanyadoo.

ASTROLOGY BOOKS

The Astrology Deck: Your Guide to the Meanings and Myths of the Cosmos
by Lisa Stardust
This deck is the perfect companion to this book and can help you deepen your understanding of astrology.

The Moon Sign Guide by Annabel Gat
A tour through what your Moon sign means for your emotional landscape, home, career ambitions, friendship, and love by longtime *Vice* astrologer and author of *The Astrology of Love & Sex*.

You Were Born for This by Chani Nicholas
A modern take on classical astrological methodology using Whole Sign astrology to interpret and unlock the potential of your birth chart.

Postcolonial Astrology: Reading the Planets through Capital, Power, and Labor
by Alice Sparkly Kat

In a cross-cultural approach to understanding astrology as a magical language, Alice Sparkly Kat unmasks the political power of astrology, showing how it can be channeled as a force for collective healing and liberation.

ASTROLOGY PODCASTS

Anne Ortelee's Weekly Weather

My personal favorite and an excellent source for the weekly astrological transits and happenings in the sky.

Ghost of a Podcast

A weekly advice podcast through the lens of astrology. Hosted by astrologer Jessica Lanyadoo.

Stars Like Us

Hosted by celebrity astrologer Aliza Kelly, this weekly podcast explores mythology, magick, and pop culture. It's one part astrology school and one part talk show.

Index

· · · · · · · · · · · · ·

Page numbers in *italics* indicate illustrations, figures, and charts.

worksheet, *63*

planets, 10. *See also* aspects;
    specific planets
    four dignities and position
      of, 163, *164*
    houses relation to, 25, *26*
    inner, 87–105
    outer, 121–39
    retrogrades in, 164–65
    social, 107–19
    symbols/glyphs, *140*

Pluto, 134–39
    characteristics and symbol,
      134, *140*
    four dignities and, *164*
    Scorpio (modern) ruled
      by, 54, 71
    worksheet, 139

Prince (musician), 171, *171*

S

Sagittarius
    Ascendant, 82
    characteristics and symbols,
      15, *17*, *18*, 20, 21,
      21, 56, *141*
    house ruled by, *15*,
      17, 31, 56
    Jupiter as ruler of, 56, 72
    Jupiter in, 110–11
    Mars in, 103
    Mercury in, 91
    Moon sign, 72
    Neptune in, 131
    Pluto in, 137
    Saturn in, 116
    Sun sign, 56

Uranus in, 125
Venus in, 97
worksheet, *57*

Saturn, 113–18
    Aquarius classically ruled
      by, 60, 73
    Capricorn ruled by, 58, 72
    characteristics and symbol,
      113, *140*
    four dignities and, *164*
    worksheet, 118

Scorpio
    Ascendant, 81
    characteristics and
      symbols, *15*, *17*, *18*, 20,
      21, 54, *141*
    house ruled by, *15*,
      17, 30, 54
    Jupiter in, 110
    Mars and Pluto as rulers
      of, 54, 71
    Mars in, 103
    Mercury in, 91
    Moon Sign, 71
    Neptune in, 131
    Pluto in, 137
    Saturn in, 116
    Sun sign, 54
    Uranus in, 125
    Venus in, 97
    worksheet, *55*

sextiles and trines, *144*,
    144–45, *145*

signs. *See also specific signs
    and topics*

characteristics and symbols
    overview, *15*, 16–17, *17*,
    18, 18–21, *21*, 23, *141*
    four dignities relation to,
      163, *164*

squares and oppositions, *146*,
    146–47, *147*

Sun (star), 13, 14, 39, 156
    four dignities and, *164*
    Leo ruled by, 48, 70
    symbol/glyph, *140*

Sun sign, 39–64. *See also
    specific signs*
    element, modality, and
      duality of, 23
    importance and influences
      of, 13, 39
    worksheet, 64–65

T

Taurus
    Ascendant, 78
    characteristics and
      symbols, *15*, *17*, *18*, 20,
      21, 42, *141*
    house ruled by, *15*,
      17, 27, 42
    Jupiter in, 108
    Mars in, 101
    Mercury in, 89
    Moon sign, 68
    Neptune in, 129
    Pluto in, 135
    Saturn in, 114
    Sun sign, 42
    Uranus in, 123
    Venus as ruler of, 42, 78

Acknowledgments

Many thanks to the editorial and marketing teams at Zeitgeist, including Meg Ilasco, Sarah Curley, Pip Davidson, and Sally McGraw. You make the process so much fun, and I love working with you!

Special thanks to my husband, Kevin, for being so supportive and encouraging throughout this process.

About the Author

Stefanie Caponi (she/her) is a Colorado-based astrologer, tarot reader, illustrator, and best-selling author of *Guided Tarot* and *Guided Tarot for Teens*. Her work is centered around exploring shadow work, healing, and creativity, using tarot and astrology as vehicles to access the hidden realms of the self. She has been reading tarot for more than 20 years and established her business as a professional tarot reader after creating her first tarot deck, the Moon Void Tarot. She began studying astrology in 2017 and has been reading astrology professionally and writing monthly horoscopes for *Dame*, focusing on intimacy and relationships, since 2019. In addition to her work with tarot and astrology, she also illustrated the YA fiction series All Our Hidden Gifts by Caroline O'Donoghue. Stefanie is a frequent astrology expert in the media and has contributed her astro insights to Well+Good, The Everygirl, and Refinery29. Connect with Stefanie on Instagram @moonvoidtarot and at moonvoidtarot.com.

About the Illustrator

Coni Curi is a self-taught illustrator from Buenos Aires, Argentina. Her style is known as "neo-nostalgia," as she combines vintage style with nowadays topics. Besides being an illustrator, she is a tarot reader and has illustrated several tarot decks. Visit Coni on Instagram @conicuri and at conicuri.com.

Hi there,

We hope you enjoyed *Guided Astrology Workbook*. If you have any questions or concerns about your book or have received a damaged copy, please contact customerservice@penguinrandomhouse.com. We're here and happy to help.

Also, please consider writing a review on your favorite retailer's website to let others know what you thought of the book!

Sincerely,
The Zeitgeist Team

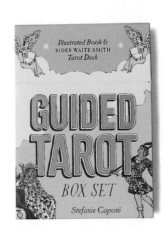

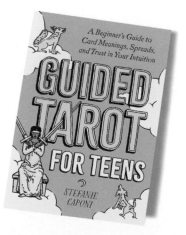